HOUSE of THOUGHTS

How Big Would Your House Be?

YVONNE BIRNELL

ISBN 979-8-89243-810-0 (paperback)
ISBN 979-8-89345-874-9 (hardcover)
ISBN 979-8-89243-811-7 (digital)

Christian Faith Publishing
832 Park Avenue
Meadville, PA 16335
www.christianfaithpublishing.com

Printed in the United States of America

I would like to dedicate this book to Love and
all the Thoughts, which invited me into their home
and shared such wonderful things with me.

CONTENTS

Foreword

Just a Thought

Ever have trouble keeping on track
When there are so many things to do?
Ever think your brain would crack
Before your day was through?

We try so hard to get things done
Then we find there is only more
Sit down and make your plans, my son
No, wait, there is someone at the door

The door of which I now do speak
Is the door within your mind
With hinges that are growing weak
For thoughts this door did find

Thoughts knock upon this battered door
They come both day and night
They insist on entrance more and more
Each bringing some kind of light

Thoughts come to us in many a way
Especially what we hear
TV, radio, or phone each day
Bringing to us joy or fear

YVONNE BIRNELL

We can block many a thought
Stop them from coming round
Just by turning the TV off
Let the phone make no sound

Be careful of what you let come in
As Jesus said we ought
Follow his rules, and you will win
Oh, yes, it's just a thought

PART 1

The House of Thoughts
Let Us Take a Trip
Together, Shall We?

1

The Trips Begin

Sharon sits at her computer, searching her notes for answers to the many questions that have been bothering her. The main question which troubled her mind tonight is who or what the power of life is. While lost in thought, she thinks she hears someone saying, "Come here. I want to show you something."

Her first thought, James, her husband, had come into the room, so she turns around, saying, "What do you need, James?" There is no one there, so she turns back to her computer, shakes her head, and continues with her thoughts again.

Again she hears the voice. Again she turns, and still there is no one. So this time, she gets up and goes to find James. "Are you calling me?"

James, who had been watching the news, turns, looks up at her, and responds with a shake of his head, "No. Why? Are you hearing those voices again?"

Sharon nods her head yes, shrugs her shoulders, and returns to her study. You would think, after all this time, Sharon would be able to tell the difference between James's voice and the ones that comes from within. The problem with Sharon is, she did not always like the voices she heard from within herself. There were too many voices which told her things that were to happen, and those things were not always good.

She goes back, sits down, and speaks with a small voice, "What do you want this time?"

The voice that comes to her is so gentle and kind this time. Sharon's discomfort and fear soon flee from her. Then the voice clearly says, "Come, my child, I have a place to show you. You have been searching for a long time for this place. Now I want to show you the way there."

As Sharon's mind starts to follow the sound of the voice, her eyes suddenly grow very heavy and finally close as she feels herself shooting toward the stars above.

Now, as she opens her eyes again, she sees a marvelous landscape, with towering trees and lovely flowers. As she looks around, she realizes there is something different about this place. The leaves on that oak trees are so vibrantly alive, more than she had ever seen before. *Wow, look at those flowers*, she thinks as she takes in the tulips, roses, all the so many diverse kinds of flowers. The aroma is so calming to her mind. *I have never seen such beautiful, vivid colors*, reminding her of almost neon colors. There are all the color combinations her mind can imagine, but they seem to be alive. The beauty here is literally breathtaking to her.

As she is taking in the beauty, she suddenly notices the light. *There is something different about this light*, her mind thinks. *Wow! This light is so bright, yet it does not hurt my eyes. And the temperature here—I just know it should be extremely hot, but the air feels so comfortable. How can this be?*

As Sharon looks around her new surroundings, she notices just how different things are here, wherever here is. Suddenly she finds herself speaking aloud, "Everything here seems to be alive." She thinks she hears giggles coming from somewhere. She looks around but sees no one. *Could it be the trees and flowers or even the rocks giggling?* her mind wonders.

She just knows the beauty she finds here in this place is more than she can totally comprehend. *The light*, she thinks, *must be the cause of all the plants here seeming to be alive.*

As she continues to stand there, many questions begin coming to her mind, questions like, where am I, and how did I get here? As she continues to look around, she spots something new that grabs her attention. There, off to the right, is a small path. She finds herself drawn to that path, as if the path were actually calling her.

Just about then, she jumps, for she hears a strange voice saying, "Mr. Think at your service."

Sharon spins around to find that the strange voice goes with an equally strange little man. His face wrinkles with age, and he looks to Sharon like he has lived a few thousand years or more. As for those clothes he wears, the dark color of the suit looks older than dirt yet still exceptionally clean and proper. Her focus then goes immediately to his eyes; there is something different about them. She cannot quite put her finger on it, but she knows in her heart, he is no threat.

After he sees he has her attention, he says, "Mr. Think at your service, Miss Sharon, just follow the path to the house. and all will be just fine."

Sharon says in total amazement, "House? What house?" With that, she turns and looks up the path; there is suddenly the biggest house Sharon has ever seen. *Now where did that come from?* she wonders. *I did not notice that grandiose thing a few minutes ago.* Sharon turns to ask the little man about the house, but he is already gone.

Sharon's mind starts racing with questions like, what did he say his name was, and where am I? About that time, she hears the first voice again. She finds herself drawn back from her thoughts to the path in front of her. Then that familiar, gentle voice speaks again, "Come, my child, this is the place you have been looking for. All the answers you seek are here."

Sharon starts up the path to the big house in front of her. When she makes her way nearer, she finds herself stopping for a moment to take in the splendor of the old house. Sharon cannot recall ever seeing a house this big, even in the magazines. As she is looking, she notices that there are clouds that seem to hover around the top of this splendid old house. How could she have missed this big of a house? Finally, curiosity takes a hold of her hand, and she continues toward the house.

There is such a welcome feeling coming to her from that old house. It is as if the house is in fact beckoning hers to enter. She finds herself looking forward to finding out about the occupants.

When she reaches the porch, she notices there are many chairs, and this causes Sharon to wonder just how many people live here. Reminded of what the voice had said, she moves on toward the door of the old house, thinking, finally she will find the answers to all her questions. Sharon just cannot visualize though that all her answers could lie in a house. You see, she has no clue to what kind of house she is entering.

Do you?

Do You Hear

There is a voice so soft and sweet
Calling you—it wants to meet
It's calling now, both night and day
Saying, Follow me; I know the way

I heard that voice myself one day
From deep within this body of clay
I cannot say how long it called
For I was stuck behind a brick wall

At first, I trembled great in fear
For who could find me hid in here
I was hiding, oh, yes, indeed
I did not like this thing called me

I'm too fat and, oh, so short
That is why I built this fort
This voice said it did understand
It had come to hold my hand

HOUSE OF THOUGHTS

As the voice spoke, my fear did melt
It seemed to know just how I felt
Brick by brick, my walls came down
For sweet and soothing was the sound

Like a voice I had never heard
Love stood there as God's word
Then He put His hand in mine
Said just believe things will be fine

The more I hear, the more I find
I have peace now in my mind
If someday you hear that sweet voice
I pray you also make this choice

2

Arrival

As Sharon steps onto the porch, she now hears a feminine voice speaking to her. "Hello, young lady, and welcome! So nice to see you have finally made the journey. Mr. Think told me you were coming up the path, so I made time out of my busy schedule to be here and greet you personally."

Sharon looks up to see a woman, who at once reminds her of the pictures she had seen in children's books, Mrs. Santa Claus. With gray hair and a jolly face, she thinks all that is missing is the red dress and a white apron.

As Sharon's mind is thinking along these lines, she hears, "What is that you are thinking?"

Sharon looks a little surprised, so Mrs. Thought reassures her, "Yes, my dear, I hear all thoughts. I can hear everything you think. For example, besides you thinking I look like Mrs. Santa, you also would like to know where you are. You have many questions running through that head of yours. First things first. Let me tell you. You have made your way to my house, which we all here call the House of Thoughts. My name is of course Mrs. Thought, and I am so glad you have come to visit us.

"What is that you're thinking now? You have never heard of this place or of me before? That is okay. Most people never take the time to get to know us. I can tell by all the questions in your head, you will learn very quickly if you will just slow those thoughts of yours down and take them one at a time.

"I also know you are wondering how many live here. I can tell you there are many residents, and you will find most of us that live here listed in a book called Webster's book of who's who, if you know what I mean.

"I can also tell you have a lot of questions you want to ask, but please come in and sit with me for a minute, and maybe I can answer some of your immediate questions by first explaining a little about Mr. Think and myself. Later on, we can talk about the others who live here.

"Like I said earlier, we are listed in Webster's book. And sometimes I forget, there are some people who do not read him very much anymore. If you wish, I can tell you what he says about Think and Thought, or you may go and get his book yourself, which sets in the main hall of the house, and look us up."

Sharon, very beleaguered by all her new surroundings, thinks, *Please, lady, just tell me what Webster says.*

Mrs. Thought gently replies, "Okay, I do not mind telling you. First, let us start with what he says about me: '*Thought*—the product of mental activity, a single act or process of thinking.' There you go, this is what he says about me. To explain further, you have to think to facilitate a thought. Now, as I said earlier, this here is my house.

"Now, on to what Webster says about Think: '*Think*—to have a conscious mind, capable of reasoning, remembering, and making rational decisions.' I hope this helps you comprehend a little further about who we are and how you got here."

Mrs. Thought proceeds to tell Sharon about the house. "Like I said earlier, we have many residents here at the House of Thoughts, and we will try and make you feel welcome during your visit. I went ahead and reserved a room here for you. You may use the room anytime you come and visit. I hope it will be satisfactory for you. Please feel free to come and go as you wish. Oh, by the way, everybody has been looking forward to the chance of meeting with you and telling you all about themselves."

Mrs. Thought, seeing the look on Sharon's face and hearing the thoughts running through her head, decides the best way to slow her down a bit is to take her mind on a different path for a little while.

"Now, may I take a little time and inform you a little of what I know about you?"

Sharon just looks at her and nods, so Mrs. Thought continues, "Let me see. First, I know you have become a seeker of truth. You feel like you want to be a better example for your family about which is the right way for them to go. Lately, you feel as if you have been going around in circles, and I heard you have been asking for help in your search. Tonight, you heard Love's voice and finally answered the call, and so here you are. Does that about cover things?"

Sharon's expression tells Mrs. Thought that she has hit the nail square on the head, so she continues, "Now, Sharon, would you like to see your room before you meet the residents?" Sharon gives a nod to indicate the answer is yes. Sharon and Mrs. Thought rise from their chairs, on the porch, and they begin their walk toward the front door.

Before they enter, Mrs. Thought takes Sharon by the arm ever so gently and speaks. "I would like to give you a piece of advice, my dear, if I may. Please take frequent breaks, and try not to stay too long in one place. We really have some big talkers here, and they will try to take all your time if you let them. Now let us take a deep breath, and when you are ready, we shall meet some amazing residents." Finally, they enter into the House of Thoughts. Let us enter with them, shall we?

On the way through the door, Mrs. Thought pats Sharon on the arm and says, "This can be such a wonderful place for some but also a scary place for others, but I want you to remember one thing: I am always just a thought away."

3

Meeting Some Residents

Mrs. Thought takes Sharon by the hand, and their tour of the house now begins. Just inside the big doors, past the entryway at the first room, Mrs. Thought turns and says, "This is Mr. Think's room, but I want to let you know that he is always very busy and not in his room very much at all."

"Do you remember him, my dear?" The look on her face prompts Mrs. Thought to reply. "He is the one who met you at the path this morning. He is what you might call our foremost greeter. You may think of him at any time then go down and speak to him. But as far as trying to catch him in his room, now that can be a hard job."

Moving on down the hall, they come to Mrs. Thought's office, which has her name right on the door. "Please feel free to come and see me whenever you need. Your room is right down the hall here."

They come to a door marked SELF as Mrs. Thought says, "This is your room, Sharon."

As they enter the room, Sharon notices the purple color of the walls—not just one shade, mind you, but all shades. She falls in love with the room immediately. She then notices that there is only a table and chair in the room. On the table is a stack of notebooks and many pencils in a beautiful container. Sharon sits in the chair and realizes she can just sit here for hours.

Mrs. Thought can tell she has done right with the color and is incredibly pleased with herself. "Why don't you just relax, and I will return to you when you let me know you are ready."

Sharon returns a smile as she sits at the desk.

Sharon immediately takes a pen in hand and starts writing notes to herself, "Breathe, Sharon. Just breathe, and slow down your mind. You have come this far. Now relax and enjoy." Over and over again Sharon writes this until she actually starts to relax.

After letting Sharon take in her surroundings, Mrs. Thought returns and asks, "Are you ready to meet some of our residents?"

Sharon nods a pleasant yes, and off they go down a long corridor and around the corner and finally come into a great, big, enormous open space. Sharon finally finds her voice and asks, "Wow, what kind of room is this?"

At that, Mrs. Thought smiles, for she now knows Sharon has completely relaxed, so she responds, "This is called the parlor. This is where the residents spend most of their time. Even though they each have their own room, they really enjoy each other's company and mingle here most of the time.

"Please! Let me remind you of what I said earlier: Do not stay too long in any one place, especially in this room. You see, when all the thoughts get together, it can be overwhelming in here at times."

Mrs. Thought proceeds by pointing out a close group of residents and calling them over. "Now let me introduce you to a few of our residents."

First in line is a tall, slender man, which gives the appearance of total peace and gentleness. Mrs. Thought starts with him and says, "Sharon, this is Love. He is my major, commanding thought around here, and I wanted you to meet him first. You might say he is the head of all groups."

Then Mrs. Thought says, "Oh, look at the time. Sharon, would you mind if I left you with Love for the time being? I really have some things I need to deal with."

Sharon nods, and Mrs. Thought says, "Good then. For now, I will let him introduce some of the others to you."

Love reaches out, shakes Sharon's hand, which totally puts Sharon at ease, and says, "I have been looking forward to meeting you for a long time. I am looking forward to some long talks together, but for now, I would like to introduce you to some incredibly good friends of mine. This is Joy, Peace, Patience, Kindness, Goodness, Faith, Gentleness, and last but not least, Self-control."

Sharon shakes each hand and nods a "how do you do?" Love looks up and sees some others coming and says, "Now, here we also have Persuasion, Faith, Belief, Trust, and Confidence. As you can see, we do not get very far without them. You may also notice that they look a lot alike. You may even get them confused occasionally, but they do not mind at all. They really know how close together their meanings are. These we call very important action thoughts."

Now, no more than a step or two later, there is another group. Love speaks and says, "Sharon, I would like to introduce you to Help and her group: Wisdom, Grace, Mercy, Hope, Knowledge, and Understanding. They are our biggest main helps in this house. When the time comes, Wisdom, Grace, Mercy, Hope, and Understanding will help you along the way. All you need to do is just ask."

Mrs. Thought just then returns and takes Sharon's arm again and says to the group, "That is enough for now. You will all have time to visit with her later. We do not want Sharon totally overwhelmed on her first visit. Now, everybody, I need to talk with Sharon privately about a particularly important matter."

She then turns to Sharon and says, "Will you please come with me back to my office?"

Mrs. Thought politely waves the others on, while she walks to her office with Sharon following close behind her. Once inside, she closes the door behind them.

The door shuts, and Mrs. Thought leads Sharon to a big comfortable chair. "Sit down, my dear, and take a load off. I can tell by the look on your face, your brain is swimming. As I said earlier, we have many residents living here in the House of Thoughts. Excitement slipped in and has some of the residents all stirred up at the moment, but as for you, you look ready for a break. I do not want to put too much on you, knowing this is your first visit, but I did want to let you know that you may come here any time you wish.

"Now, on to that important matter I mentioned out there. I must inform you about the pathway. This morning, you met Mr. Think there, but sometimes there are other residents who travel that path, but they live down the road in another house. There are some thoughts you need to watch out for, at least until you learn how to recognize them and know how to avoid them. If it is all right with you, I am going to send Help with you. She collaborates really well with newcomers till they learn their way around.

"When you want to come again, just sit in front of your computer, and let the inner part of your mind do the job it was meant to do. And along with Help and her group, they will get you back and forth with no problems. Until the next time we meet. I bid you a fine adieu."

With this, Sharon feels a heaviness come upon her mind, which she is too exhausted to fight, and she starts to drift backward. She finds this feeling very comforting but tiring as her eyes again close.

PART 2

Was That Really Real?

1

Home Again

Sharon wakes and finds she is sitting in front of her computer. Still dazed a little by her thoughts, she wonders, *Did I really just leave my chair and enter into a new realm?*

No way, she thinks. *I must have just dosed off for a minute or two.* But then she hears herself saying aloud, "Everything seemed so real and vivid." Not to wake James, she puts her hand over her mouth. She finally thinks, *Enough! No matter what it was, I just know my brain sure feels exhausted.* Looking at the clock, she realizes, it is past midnight again.

Suddenly, her mind starts to wander off again. She starts remembering the House of Thoughts and finds herself asking questions like, Where did those thoughts come from? Is there really a House of Thoughts? Did I just actually meet Love?

Suddenly, Sharon realizes she is losing control over her thoughts again and says aloud, "Oh, no, you don't, Mind. You get back here. If I go to sleep this time, it will be in my bed. Now that is a good thought. I think I will go to bed and sleep on this for a while."

Sharon starts to turn off her computer but sees these words going across her screen, which stops her in her tracks. It reads, "Sharon, do not forget about us. We are waiting for you to return. Signed Mrs. Thought."

Startled, Sharon starts to call her husband in to see the words, but all at once, they disappear. Sharon shakes her head and says, "Now I know it is time to go to bed." Therefore, with that thought behind her, she quickly shuts off the computer, and up to bed she goes.

Now I would like to ask you a question. Yes, you, the one reading this book. Do you think, if you were Sharon, you could just lie down and go right off to sleep after such an experience? If so, after your break, I hope you will join us in the next chapter.

If you cannot sleep either, come join us now.

2

Frist Interview

You see, Sharon does go upstairs and lie down; however, she soon realizes she has brought back with her too many residents from the House of Thoughts. You can say her head is getting a little crowded. She tries shaking her head, beating up her pillow and rolling back and forth, but she cannot shake these thoughts. Not wanting to wake up James, she finally gets out of bed and goes back down the stairs.

Quietly, she gets herself a drink and goes to her study, turns on the light, and sits in her big chair. Looking up, she sees her computer and says, "I am not turning you back on, not yet at least." Maybe a pencil and paper will work for now. So with pencil and paper in hand, she now turns back to the thoughts that would not let her sleep.

Speaking as Mrs. Thought had told her to, to the inner part of her mind, she says, "Let's go slow here. I do not want to be up all night, fighting with all you, thoughts, I seemed to have carried back with me."

Then she speaks, "Help, I also am asking, please come and do your part. Now let's get started, but please one at a time."

Sharon takes a deep breath and realizes that Help has brought with her Peace and Wisdom. She now feels better and more able to manage the job ahead.

"Okay, Mind, where do we begin?" Before she finishes the question, Mind has ushered in the first thought for her to deal with. *Now this is nice,* she thinks as the memory of her actually getting to meet Love comes into focus. The thought becomes so real; she just knows Love, himself, has followed her back home. She feels Warmth and Comfort spread over her whole body.

"Oh, Love, what wonderful thoughts you bring to me. I want to let you know, I have heard about you before, but they just have not done you justice."

Instantly, Sharon finds herself on the porch of the House of Thoughts and standing right in front of Love. Love then speaks to Sharon and says, "Come and let me tell you the truth about myself. Before I go too far into our talk, there is something I need to tell you. So many people get me confused with Lust. I know that we look the same at first. But just wait, and Lust will show his true colors. I would like you to know the truth about me personally. Maybe then you can let others know.

"People really need to understand the difference between Love and Lust. Love is the ruler of the Spirit realm. Lust rules over the realm of flesh. Love gives, and Lust takes.

"I have to admit, when people first met Lust, he does seem to give, but that is only to get them hooked, you know, as you when you give some kind of bait to fish to lure them in so you can take their life to feed your pleasure. Lust destroys people's lives every day, and the only way to save them from him is through words of Truth, which I am here to share with you."

Love looks at Sharon with such passion. Sharon softly asks, "What does Webster say about you?"

Love just smiles and says, "Go look. He says a lot, but you may pick your favorite."

Sharon looks up Love and finds out there are nineteen different definitions. As the reader of this book, if you want to, you may go to *Webster* and read all of them. I, as the writer, have picked out just one of them for Sharon to dwell on. Now listed here in the book, *Webster* says, **Love** is a profoundly tender, passionate affection for others.

"Yes, Sharon, as it is written. Greater love hath no man than this, that a man lay down his life for his friends," Love gently speaks.

Sharon turns back to Love and asks, "What does *profoundly*, *tender*, and *passionate* mean?"

"Look them up," comes the response from Love.

Therefore, Sharon picks up the book and says, "Here goes. Webster says, *Passionate*—having, compelled by or ruled by intense emotion or strong feeling.

"*Profoundly*—showing deep insight or understanding, originating in the depths of ones being, going beyond what is superficial or obvious."

When Sharon comes to the word *tender*, she finds three separate times the word *tender*, written with different meaning groups for each time the word is there. After reading all the different meanings, she finally chooses this one: *Tender*—easily moved to sympathy or compassion.

"Wow! Look, Love, the more I look up, the more questions I find coming into my mind," Sharon says with a smile.

Love can see Sharon's eyes growing tired. So Love says, "This is enough for tonight, Sharon. Tomorrow is another day, and right now you need your sleep. While you sleep, think about what you have just read. That way, you will keep the other thoughts from bothering you. Good night, Sharon. I will see you in the morning."

Does It Matter

A thousand words is a picture's worth
We've thousands of pictures here on earth
Now with words, I pray you will see
A picture of what words are to me

Now your words have a way of showing
Right through the flesh, they are glowing
Producing pictures to all who look
Ever feel like your life's an open book?

YVONNE BIRNELL

Does it matter which words you use?
Your words will give about you clues
Words let others inside you see
Let others see what you believe

Now once your words you start to speak
To others you show if you are weak
Or they will see that all along
In your belief, you are very strong

Yes, it matters how we use a word
With a word, we produce bad or good
Idol words will not form a thing
Except you will stand before the King

3

New Day, New Thought

Sharon wakes to find James gone again. She rubs her eyes and sits up on the side of the bed, wondering when the last time she and James had to share a morning together. James always makes it a habit to kiss her goodbye every morning, but she still misses their time of watching the news, talking about their coming day, and having coffee together.

Oh, coffee, Sharon remembers. James is also exceptionally good at making sure she has a fresh hot pot of coffee when she wakes up. She speaks aloud, "God, thank You for blessing me with that man of mine," and down the stairs, she goes to get some coffee.

With coffee in hand, she heads for her study as memories fill her mind of what Love had said last night. She is ready for more of what Love has to share with her so she can share the wonderful information with James and the rest of her family. You see, James always seems to be spellbound when he is listening to Sharon's tales of innovative words she learns, and she enjoys sharing her innovative words with him.

With coffee in hand and settled in her chair, her mind goes back to what Love, before telling her good night, had said, to think about all the definitions she had read, the ones about Love, Passionate,

Tender, and Profound. Questions keep coming to her mind, but she wants to go slow. You see, she wants everything together in the right order.

Let us see here, she thinks, *which is the best way to say this: True love is profoundly tender and passionate. That seemed fine to say if the other person knew what all the words meant. Another way a person could put the meaning of true love is having your life guided by intense feelings of sympathy and compassion for others, coming from the very depths of ones being.*

Sharon can feel Excitement, bouncing around inside her. She just has to talk with Love and tell him what she herself has figured out. Now Sharon is ready to go again to the House of Thoughts.

Yes, Excitement, or what feels like excitement, has gotten a hold of her, and so quickly she turns on her computer and stares at the screen, thinking of the wonderful place she had gone last night. Her mind is telling her, "Yes, a place where everything had seemed so much more alive." She is remembering the way the sun had shined brightly but was not too hot. In addition, she remembers the feeling she had, that if she talked first, the flowers would talk back. Deeper and deeper, she goes into her thoughts, and soon finds herself opening her eyes to the meadow again.

With Excitement leading Sharon, she runs toward the path but soon realizes something is definitely different. The sun seems less bright, even dull you might say, and extremely cold today. All the colors, which she had seen yesterday, looks very gray and lifeless today.

Then suddenly, a very cold shiver starts running through Sharon. That is when she hears a strong, deep, husky voice coming from behind her, saying, "Sharon, where are you going so fast? Why not stop and talk with us for a while?"

Excitement quickly leaves Sharon, which makes her stop in her tracks and turn around. There, standing before her, she sees a tall, lanky man with a smug smile on his face.

"Who are you?" she inquires with a small shaky voice.

"Who, me? You want to know about me?" he answers with a cold laugh. "Really, Sharon, I did not think I would have to tell you. But since you have asked, I will introduce myself to you. My name is Lust. I was hoping to meet you yesterday but that Mrs. Thought stopped me. She always introduces the newcomers to Love and his group first.

"I sent Anxiety to meet you and draw you over here so I could introduce you to my group of friends."

Suddenly, Sharon realizes that what she had thought was Excitement is not Excitement after all but, in actuality, is that dreaded Anxiety.

Then Lust continues, "You see, I have learned, over the years, that people always want more once they find their way here. I have learned just to wait my turn to meet all of you. Now I would like to introduce you to a few of my friends."

Turning around, Lust calls up his horde of thoughts to come and stand next to him and proceeds to name them for Sharon. "First in line, I would like you to meet Hate and Death. Next, I would like you to meet Fear and his look-alikes, Worry, Dread, and Anxiety, which you have already had the pleasure of experiencing. Don't you think we make an effective team?"

Suddenly, Fear enters Sharon, and she feels him as she had never done before. The light around her and in her starts getting dimmer and dimmer. The cold and darkness keep increasing all around her.

Then Lust says, "Oh, you should already know Depression and how he affects people." The cold in the air is starting to fill her lungs, her very being, totally and completely. That is when this question starts coming to her mind quietly at first, then louder and louder. Is this what Death feels like? She hears a sound, like someone laughing, which reminds her of the sound, as if a person breathing their last breath. She remembers her mother had called that sound the death rattle. Sharon can feel herself slipping down into that deep darkness. Farther and farther she falls, and as she falls, she starts wondering if she would ever escape this growing madness, which is consuming her.

Then she hears that gentle voice, in urgency, saying, "Come to me, NOW, my child. Hurry and follow the sound of my voice."

Sharon starts reaching out to that voice in total desperation. Slowly at first, the coldness that had such a grip on her starts to leave her body and mind, and she can feel herself rising again.

Soon she opens her eyes and understands something clearly at last, just as if it had been the first time. There, to Sharon's surprise, is Mr. Think, saying in his strange little voice, "Think at your service. Mrs. Thought is waiting for you at the house. I brought Help and Encouragement with me to be with you."

Sharon smiles a weak but heartfelt smile toward him. She sits there and takes a couple of deep breaths, then slowly, Encouragement helps her up, and they all head for the house.

Mrs. Thought meets Sharon at the door of the big house and is ready to ask her, "Why! Didn't you let Help bring you back?" Then Mrs. Thought sees Sharon's face, and she can tell that Sharon has learned her lesson. All she can do is ask, "Are you okay?"

Sharon looks at Mrs. Thought and nods yes. Then Sharon just busts out and says, "What just happened to me and why?"

Mrs. Thought responds as calmly as she can, "You forgot what I told you last night. You forgot to keep Help with you to bring you back."

All of a sudden, Memory comes flooding back to Sharon about what Mrs. Thought has told her. Along with the memories come Guilt and Condemnation, and they hit Sharon so hard; all she can do is sit down and start crying.

Mrs. Thought quickly speaks, "Guilt, Condemnation, get on out of here right now. You and your group have done enough damage for one day." Sharon's mind cannot take it anymore; she cries out for Help to do something and just sits there and waits for Help to produce good thoughts. Hoping, Help brings Relief, and together they huddle with her.

Sharon is trying to sort out all the thoughts that are going through her mind. There are times her brain just feels like it is going to explode, and this happens to be one of those times. She thinks, *How can so many ideas fit into one small space? I must be crazy to think I can figure out any of this.*

Soon, Help summons Careful, and with him, he brings Warmth and Comfort, which surrounds Sharon, and she starts feeling more of her strength return. Then Love shows up, comes over, puts his arms around Sharon, and lifts her to her feet. Sharon is so glad to see Love that she just blurts out, "You were so right. That Lust and his group are deadly. I am so sorry, Mrs. Thought, and I definitely learned my lesson. I will keep Help and her group close at all times from here on out."

Now Joy, Peace, Gentleness, and the rest of the group has come in also to be with Sharon. Soon, Sharon is feeling her old self and remembers why she is in a hurry to get back to the House of Thoughts. After taking three or four deep breaths, she feels ready to share the definition she has put together about love. She starts telling Love about the definitions she read last night and about putting them together in an order, which gives her a new understanding of the meaning of true love.

4

Time for Belief

Love takes Sharon in his arms and tells her that she is on the right track, but now Love asks Sharon to build on this foundation and add Persuasion and Faith to her new definition. "Love, you see, without being persuaded by Love, which produces Faith, and without Faith in that Love, then Love does nobody any good. You have heard that Faith comes by hearing. Well, that is how you are persuaded. Then from being persuaded comes Belief, Trust, and Faith. It is time for you to have a long talk with Persuasion and Faith, along with their look-alikes. I know Faith is over in Belief's room. Are you ready for this?"

Sharon nods yes, and off they go.

Sharon and Love arrive at Belief's door and find Faith sitting there, waiting for them. With a voice full of cheer, Faith says, "Welcome. Come on in. Have a sit. Are you ready to talk?"

Sharon nods, so Faith continues saying, "Good. Then let us talk for a while. I want to let you know I have already heard the story about what happened. I want you to know we are at your service. Sharon, please feel free to call upon us whenever you need."

Sharon replies with warm thanks.

Faith then proceeds, "Please let me tell you a little about us. Sharon, if you will look in *Webster's* book about Faith, Belief, Confidence, Persuasion, and Trust, you will find us all leading back to each other. Now, Sharon, I know you and your tendency is to lean toward Belief, which is fine with me. That is why I had Love bring you here. If it is all right with you, I will turn you over to Belief and let you two get aquatinted."

The thought of Sharon having time alone with her wonderful Belief is a comfort to her, and she has no problem displaying her emotions.

Love finally speaks up. "Now we will leave you alone with Belief and let you two have a talk."

As soon as Sharon and Belief are alone, she just has to ask her first question. "What is true belief?"

Belief takes a step backward and says, "Slow down! Let us first go and see what *Webster* says." They both go to visit *Webster*. Looking at the book together, Belief says, "Here we find *Webster* has four different meanings listed for belief, starting with 'something believed; opinion; conviction.' Then you have 'confidence in the truth of the existence of something not immediately susceptible to rigorous proof.' The third definition is where we see '*confidence*, then *faith*, *trust*: children's *belief* in parents.' Now onto the fourth and final definition, we find 'a religious creed or faith.'"

Belief turns to Sharon and says, "Let's look back at number three. This is where we see four of us words joined together. Remember, we started with me, Belief, and there we find Confidence, Faith, Trust, and myself. Remember in the parlor, Love said we four were look-alikes. So then, when people have belief, they can also say they have confidence in, have faith in, or trust in something, right?"

To answer the question, Sharon says, "Yes. Then you, Belief, are one of those words people cannot live without in their life. Even if they say they do not believe, they still believe that they do not believe. You cannot stop yourself from believing in something. Even if that something is nothing to others, it is still something the individual believes in, right?"

Sharon does not wait for an answer. She pushes on and asks Belief, "Now, where does Belief come from?"

Belief tells her, "It comes by hearing words spoken to them or reading words that have been written. Our top leader is Persuasion. Words are used to persuade people one way or another. Either you can hear and believe, or you may see and believe. You can also, as they say, here from within, believe and then see."

Sharon finally says, "Boy, I am getting confused. If it is all right with you, I need to go and break this down a little. I will come back later, okay, Belief?"

Sharon wakes again in her study and turns off her computer and goes to work on her house. As she cleans, she starts thinking, *Maybe if I take my mind off these thoughts for a while, I might be able to get my mind to rest.*

Trying to busy herself with the issues of her physical house, she looks around and thinks, *First, I will get the dishes done then sweep the floor.* She picks up a dish and moves to put it in the sink, but her mind does not let her stop thinking of the question that she had last asked Belief.

Finally, she gives up on her house and picks up her pencil and paper to write, *Now, if you believe you are, then you are, right? So then, if you do not believe, what are you?* Wait, I know everybody exists, whether they believe in anything or not. I know this because I have met people that do not think they are anything, and still they are here. As she sits, she remembers her mother saying, "Oh, don't worry about me. I am nothing to you." The thought comes to her. *Did Mom really mean that, or was she just trying to get me to realize she is something to me? Which way do I go?* her mind wonders. *Okay, let us try again. First, Belief said he comes from hearing and hearing what somebody says, like the report that says the earth is round. Then he said you could also get belief from seeing a picture of the earth being round. So I could safely say, either hearing or seeing could bring Belief to a person.* After thinking about this for a while, she feels like things in her mind are straightening out.

Now, being comfortable with the hearing and seeing part, Sharon decides to move on to the next thing Belief had said.

Belief had then said a person can say, "I believe like Christopher Columbus," who conceived a thought about the earth being round. He set out to prove what he believed. Did Chris have somebody telling him the earth was round? I cannot say, for I was not there. I believe he got his belief from a thought, according to my history books, which says he did have many people telling him he was crazy for even thinking that way.

Back to the computer Sharon goes, "Maybe this time I will figure out all of this. If I call in Wisdom and Understanding to be with me, I believe I can."

Sharon remembers to call Help this time to take her back to see Belief. When she arrives at the house, there is no one to meet her at the door, so off she goes to Belief's room again. Belief greets Sharon with a smile and listens as she speaks and tells Belief what she has figured out.

Sharon then remembers her companions, "Belief, may we ask for Wisdom and Understanding to stay with us before I ask the next question?"

Belief nods yes.

Then Sharon proceeds with the next question, "What good are beliefs?"

Belief asks Sharon to remember what her dad had always said.

"You have to stand for something, or you will fall for anything."

"He was talking about beliefs. You have to stand for your beliefs, or you will fall under the burden of everybody's belief. Let me try to put an example here for you. Let us say you go to the store and get supplies for your household for the week, and the clerk tells you, you owe $50. If you have belief in that store's system, you will pay the clerk, have no second thought about it, and walk out of the store with your things. You fill yourself with belief and leave no room for doubt.

"If you believe the clerk is wrong, you may or may not ask them to check the prices again. There are people who believe that to question the clerk is not worth taking the time and will pay anyway. On the other hand, there are those who believe the chance of robbery is wrong in any form and will fight all the way. They believe a wrong is wrong, even if it is over a penny.

"Do you see how many ways there are to go with your belief? Now add on the situation of not having strong belief, and your friend starts pushing his belief on you, which is vastly different from yours. Let us say, you are shy, so you would not ask any questions, but your friend, who was watching, insists that you ask for a recheck. What are you to do, believe in your shyness or go with your friend's Belief. Do you see how confusing a situation could become if you do not stand up for your own belief? You see, by the example, we are led through life by what we believe. People react differently to situations because of the way they believe or *who* they believe.

"Did you know, some people change their beliefs all the time? I like to say to those people, 'Don't you feel like you are going crazy, like you are a ship tossed about by stormy waves on the open sea?'"

About that time, Love and Faith show back up in the room. Sharon's mind starts to swim, and she looks at Belief, says thank you for all the information, and then asks if they would mind if she left for a while. Everyone agrees that would be a promising idea. Therefore, with goodbyes out of the way, Sharon closes her eyes once more and leaves.

Wow, what a trip, she thinks, for she has just come back again from the House of Thoughts. Sharon looks at the clock and sees that three hours had passed this time. She realizes that she is definitely ready for a break. Therefore, Sharon turns off the computer and decides it is time for a long, hot soak in the tub.

As Sharon soaks in the hot water, she concludes, to have less confusion in her life, she needs to be careful what words or thoughts she lets enter into her mind.

PART 3

This Is Real Enough for Me

1

Time to Share

Today, she takes a little extra time with the things that make a woman feel like a woman. She enjoys an extra splash of perfume and brings out the silky undergarments. Now that she feels refreshed, she is ready to get the dishes done and the floor cleaned.

James will be home soon, and dinner will be on time tonight for a change. She realizes she can think and clean at the same time. Oh, how she loves James, she does not even want to, cannot even if she tries to, and will not even if she can, ever think of being without James. To Sharon, James is especially important in her life. Especially since their children now, all grown with families of their own, they just do not need her as much.

Tonight will be special for her and James. After dinner, maybe they can sit in front of the fireplace and have a nice talk. Sharon is looking forward to telling James all about her trip to the House of Thoughts and meeting all the wonderful residents there.

While still in thought, Sharon hears James's truck pull into the drive. Within minutes, James is in the house, and Sharon is throwing her arms around his neck, asking, "How was your day, dear? Are you hungry?"

James hugs Sharon and replies, "I'm starved. What's for supper?"

Sharon smiles and says, "Food. Is that all right with you?"

They both laugh and head off to eat.

After dinner, Sharon asks, "James, have you ever had the chance to just sit and think?"

James shrugs his shoulder, but she continues, "What kind of questions goes through your mind?"

James looks lovingly at Sharon and asks, "Where are you going with this, my dear? Have you learned something new, and you need to talk with somebody again?" James holds out his arms, and Sharon goes to him, nodding yes. "Okay, let's talk then." James leads Sharon into the living room, where they sit together in front of the fireplace.

Sharon begins to ramble, "I wonder, James, do other people have the same problem I have? Do you think they can keep their minds on one subject longer than I do? Oh, so many times I wish I could just shut my mind off. Every time I think that way, my brain then inquires of me, who would turn me back on if you did?"

James responds quickly, "Slow down there a minute, Honey. Is this a question-and-response session? For if it is, then I can tell you, I think everyone has problems with their minds becoming too full."

Sharon shakes her head, so James comes back with, "Or is this one of those questions and me just listening session?"

Sharon says, "I'm sorry, dear. I guess I am a little excited about all I have learned lately. Please just jump in anywhere and comment on what I am saying. That way, you can slow me down and maybe chase Excitement off, so I won't forget where I am going.

"I have had so many questions going through my mind for the last couple of days. I actually thought I was going to go crazy. Then I heard that voice last night. Remember I asked you if you were calling me? Anyway, I ended up going to this wonderful place, where the flowers and trees and even the rocks looked like they would speak, if I had talked to them first, that is. Then there was this house I found and this woman I met called it the House of Thoughts. I met these thoughts there, which looked just like people, and I even talked with them."

James comes in with, "You did what? Where? With whom? Honey, please slow down. We have all night if necessary."

Sharon takes a deep breath and slowly continues, "Okay, let's try it this way: I wrote down some things about my trip on the computer. If you do not mind, I would like you to go and read about my adventure. Then when you come back, we can talk about what I feel like I have learned."

James sees the excitement in her eyes and responds lovingly, "I think that sounds like a wonderful idea. Why not just sit and relax while I read what you wrote. I will be back in a little while, okay?"

Sharon nods, and off James goes to her study.

James comes back about an hour later with, "Wow, how do people put that? Looks like you must have taken a trip and not left the farm. That is extremely powerful stuff you wrote today. Now I think I know a little bit of where you are coming from." Then James takes a deep breath and continues. "Now, shall we continue? I think I would like to listen for a while." James takes a seat next to Sharon and listens as she begins.

Sharon starts with, "What you read, my dear, is my adventures of yesterday evening, which I think turned into an all-night-and-day session. Now I would like to share with you the answers I have found along the way. This is not to say I am right, but maybe, just maybe, I am closer than I was yesterday.

"Let's start with the difference between love and lust. I mean, what I got out of that conversation with Love. They are hard to tell apart when you first encounter them. But as I found out personally, when you actually met them face-to-face, boy, they are as different as night and day. People need to learn that love comes from the inside out, and lust comes from the outside in. Do you see what I mean, James?"

James just shakes his head and says, "That sounds hard to do. You see, once something is inside you, how do you know which way it came?"

Sharon gives him that look, so James continues, "Okay, for an example, let us say you see a car, and you find yourself wanting that car. Which would you say you have, love or lust?"

Sharon speaks up. "James, don't you see the difference? Lust's way is from you seeing a car and just having to have that car for yourself, with no thought for others. Then on the other hand, love is a thought, which comes to you. If I had a car, I sure could help all those people who need rides."

James shakes his head and says, "Now I understand. It depends on which way you perceive things. One way is being selfish, and one way being helpful, right?"

Sharon comes back with, "That's right, honey. That is a very good way of putting the situation. That reminds me of what Love told me last night. Love gives, and lust takes. Lust comes in and tries to take over, making a person selfish. In the process, lust tries destroying love, which wants to live in them. Love, on the other hand, according to *Webster*, comes from deep within a person and enjoys giving. Now I see why Love also said, 'We need to put faith and belief into this equation.' The way a person is taught or believes will determine how they will react to a situation."

James asks, "What do you mean?"

Sharon says, "James, remember reading my conversation with Belief? Remember, belief comes by hearing words that are spoken or reading the written word. If people are not taught about love, how can they believe love lives inside them? How can they know what is to govern their lives?"

"Okay, if faith comes by hearing, then how is a person supposed to know whom to believe?" James responds.

Sharon stops in her tracks and looks at James for a moment then says, "I guess everyone starts learning from their parents or the adults in their lives. You know adopted children do not know they are adopted until someone tells them. That is how families continue traditions from one generation to the next. Problems do not start until children get to go out into the rest of the world and find out other people live different, or lust enters a child, like when Cain slew Able. I mean, if they see others have things different than they do and are having fun. that is when the trouble begins."

"Honey, do you remember when we got together? You had come from a small family, and I came from a large family. You were nervous about all those people being around, but I, on the other hand, enjoyed them because I had all those years of hearing Mom and Dad telling and showing me how to love my brothers and sisters. Love told me it was written, so I went and looked up what he said. I found the verse **John 15:13**: 'Greater love hath no man than this, that a man lay down his life for his friends.' Does that help?"

James says, "A little, I guess. I can see you have given lots of time about what you have learned today. I want to thank you for sharing all this with me."

Sharon looks lovingly at James and finally says, "Honey, I am really tired. Thank you for listening to me tonight. I think I am ready for bed. Do you think we could continue this tomorrow?"

With that, James stands and extends a hand to Sharon, and they head off to bed.

PART 4

Questions Need Answers

1

Meeting Experience

Sharon and James have a wonderful time in the coming weeks. They try out the new concepts Sharon has learned at the House of Thoughts. They start checking their desires to see if they are coming from the inside of themselves or coming from things they see and hear.

Then one night, Sharon falls asleep quickly, but her sleep is not peaceful, for a question James had asked her would not leave her mind. How do we know whom and what to believe? She starts thinking in her dream, *I need to go back to the House of Thoughts and speak to someone.*

Soon she is standing on the front porch of the house, and Mrs. Thought is saying, "Hello, I am glad you remembered I was only a thought away. Come on in. Love is expecting you and has a friend he wants you to meet. I have set up my office so you could have some private time."

Sharon follows Mrs. Thought into her office and finds Love standing there with a friend.

"Sharon, I would like for you to meet Experience and his friend Understanding. They are the ones who reveal the Real Truth concerning a person's Faith, Belief, Confidence, and Trust, which we

43

already know come from what they hear or see. Now, before I get too far ahead of myself, shall we go and see what *Webster* says about them?"

After looking up Experience in *Webster* and finding four different meanings, Sharon sees this definition for *Experience*: 'knowledge or practical wisdom gained from what one has observed, encountered, or undergone.' Now to Understanding: 'to *put together*, that is (mentally) to *comprehend*; by implication, to consider, understand, be wise.'

Sharon turns and asks if she could sit for a minute. Everyone agrees after looking at her face and seeing that the blood, which should have been there, has left her face completely. Sharon sits down and takes a couple of deep breaths, letting them out slowly.

Love is the first to speak, saying, "I know this is a hard part of your journey, but I also know you can manage this. I want you to know, we will go as slow as need be, so take your time and ask all the questions you want. This part of the mission is what I like to call the pulling together and looking deep."

Experience steps up and says, "You know, I have been with you all your life, and now you will find out just how I have been working for you. If it is all right with you, I would like to call in Faith, Belief, Confidence, and Trust."

Sharon just nods, for right now, her voice has left her, and she has no strength.

"All right, now that everyone is present, we can proceed." Experience comes over to Sharon and says, "You use me to go through life. By your faith, you lead me, which in turn leads you. You cannot change the way I go until you change the way you believe.

"As Love told you earlier, I am what you might call your faith meter, and Understanding comes when you put us all together. Do you remember when you and James were having trouble with your finances? I will now explain to you why.

"I would like you to go back a few years, to the root or main reason of your problem. You see, you never believed in credit because of the way your parents taught you. They said that if you wanted something, you had to work until you had the money or completed the job set before you. Then you could get the thing you wanted. You did not have the saying like, 'I will give you this now, then you can do this to earn it.' Your parents had a separate way of dealing with you than other parents did with their children. They found things you wanted and put them in front of you and said, 'Now if you want this, I am requiring you to do this to get it.' Let me give you an example if I may, which might help you understand.

"Sharon, I want you to remember when you were five years old and when you found that two-foot walking doll, in the store. Remember how much you wanted that doll, but she cost seven dollars, which you did not have, nor did you have any thought in your little mind, like 'How do I get seven dollars?' Remember, Sharon, how you kept talking about that doll all the time? Then one day, your dad said, 'If you want her, I will make a deal with you. If you go a whole week without any accidents, I will give you a dollar. Then after you save half the price of the doll and if you still want her, I will go in with you and get the doll for you. How does that sound with you?'

"I remember how thrilled you were and how you believed and had set your mind on getting that doll. You believed very strongly that you could achieve the mission that had been set in front of you."

"This is where I come in. You see, by having that kind of belief and drawing strength from the joy of those thoughts of achieving your goals, you had put some very tight reigns on me. What else could I do? Your faith was leading me in everything you experienced."

Sharon starts smiling as memories begin to flood over her. She has not thought about that big doll for many years. Then she remembers, *Hey, that is the doll I fixed up for Melody when she got married.* You see, Melody was Sharon's only daughter. When Sharon had lost her mother, her dad asked her to help clean the house and sort things out. While cleaning the house, they came across that old doll, all dirty and stuffed into a box out on the back porch. It just happened that dolls name was Melody also. Sharon had thought it would be great to clean up and dress the old doll, which had meant so much to her and give the doll to her daughter for a wedding gift.

There is a sound, as if someone clearing his or her throat, in the room, and Sharon finally remembers that she is in the middle of a conversation with Experience. She looks up to see everyone smiling back at her, which really puts Sharon at ease.

Love, again, is the first to speak, "I am so glad you have some wonderful memories connected with that doll, but we have a lot of ground to cover tonight, and we need to move on, if that is all right with you."

Sharon responds happily with a yes, and now Experience takes the floor back.

"As I was saying earlier, Sharon, your belief, in your ability to achieve your goal, guided me on which way I should go. Maybe this will make things clearer for you."

"Let's say you have to go to the store and be back home by nightfall, but you live twenty miles away. Your first thought is about all the ways there are to achieve your goal. First, you think the only way there is to walk, but then you realize you have a horse outside. First, belief/decision: Can I walk there and back before dusk, or would it be better to ride the horse? You decide to ride the horse to town. Why? Because you believe you will get to town and back quicker.

"Now you go out and saddle the horse, jump up on his back, and take off toward town. Your experiences, on the way, will depend on how much you believe you can get the job done. If you are completely convinced you can, you will act like it. What I mean is, you will hold those reigns tight and not let the horse veer off track. If doubt enters your mind, the horse will know, and he will start fighting with you. The more doubt and fear you have, the longer and more violent the fight will become. Do you see what I mean?"

Sharon looks around the room, and she can tell by the sincere looks on their faces that they are trying to help her. She finally speaks, "If it is all right with you guys, I would like to tell you want I think I have heard here tonight. You see, when I hear something for the first time, it has a tendency to get jammed up in my brain, and so if I talk about it, to me it is like taking the ideas and moving them to their proper place."

Everyone just smiles, and Love says, "We understand. Please feel free to take the floor and do your thing so to speak."

Sharon stands and starts walking back and forth across the floor. She seems to be thinking ridiculously hard. Finally, she speaks, "Let me see if I have this down. You say you are like a horse that takes me places, and if I believe or have confidence in what I am doing, I will treat you as if I believe, draw strength from my joy of the thoughts, which I put primarily in my mind, and hold you in check. I will only let you go where I say. But if I do not believe strongly enough, that means you might get away from my leadership and lead me into unfamiliar territory, where my confidence and trust in my own thoughts might get totally lost."

Everyone in unison speaks, "I think she's got it."

Sharon goes on, "You know something, the more we talk about Faith, the more I am realizing that separating him from his group or choosing one above the other can be very bad for my well-being. I realize now how important Understanding really is. It's one thing to know about you all, but with the experience I get by using you, I come to an understanding of how you all work together. Persuasion, Faith, Belief, Confidence, and Trust might look alike, but they still work better when you keep them all together and build one on top of the other. Persuasion is the seed that you plant. Faith is the blade, and Belief is the ear, and Trust with Confidence is the corn in the ear."

Love is now laughing with the others as he heads over to Sharon and puts his arm around her, saying, "No more thinking, you guys. I can tell you most definitely, she has got it. Now, Sharon, I would like you to take your newfound knowledge. Go home, and get some well-deserved sleep. Good night and sweet dreams."

Sharon starts to close her eyes and leave, when just then the thought came into her mind. "Wait a moment, I came here with a question, and I am not leaving without the answer. I had James ask me, how do we know whom to believe? I can't go back without being able to tell him."

Love takes Sharon in his big arms and tells her, "You already have the answer in your heart, and after you have a good night sleep, you will find it sitting there, waiting for you to put it in the right place in your mind. Now I really think you need to give your mind a rest and let things settle down. Like I said before, take your time, and keep asking yourself all those questions. Move the definitions around until they fit for you."

Sharon was definitely tired, so she agreed with Love and thought a good night sleep would not hurt her at all. With that settled, she said her goodbyes and left. Sharon knew she would have no trouble sleeping tonight with things at peace in her mind.

PART 5

What a Time Ahead

1

Time Out

Sharon awakes and finds James gone. When she looks up at the clock above her bed, there is a small alarm going off inside her. Here it is, almost three o'clock. James will be home shortly, and she is still in bed. *How long was I gone this time?* she wonders.

Oh no, the coffee. I wonder if the pot has burned up. I know I will not be drinking any of that coffee today. With that thought, she jumps out of bed and goes down the stairs. First going to the coffee-pot, she looks and sees nothing burning. *Good,* she thinks.

She decides a cold pop out of the refrigerator will do simply fine at this time of day. She grabs a soda pop and looks around the kitchen, thinking this place sure can use some cleaning. Sharon starts by putting away the dishes she had washed last night after dinner. Soon the kitchen is looking good, even if she thinks so herself.

Now I have just enough time to get some dinner made before James gets home. *I know,* she thinks, *I will fix him some Sloppy Joes. He had mentioned that we have not had those for a while, and he would surely like some.* As she starts preparing dinner, she thinks, *I hope he is not upset with me for not answering the phone when he called at lunchtime, or maybe he did not even call.* Sharon shakes her head, for she knows better than that. James calls every day at lunchtime. Why would today be any different?

As Sharon finishes preparing dinner, she hears James pull up into the driveway. She goes to the door to meet him as she usually does and throws her arms around his neck and says, "Hi, honey. How was your day? Are you hungry?"

This time she does not get the normal answer. This time James says, "My day was okay, but I really would like to hear about your night. You were gone, Sharon, I mean I thought you had died on me. Your skin, it was so cold and the only sign of life, I had was you were still breathing but barely. If I had not already known that you were taking those strange trips., well I tell you right now, I would have called 911." James realizes he is yelling at the woman he loves. So to get control of himself, he takes a deep breath, then pulls Sharon close. Almost in tears, he says, "Sorry, dear. I did not know if I would come home and find a dead body or what." Taking another deep breath, he continues, "Now, to set your mind at ease, I did not call at lunchtime because as far as I knew, when I left this morning, you were still gone."

Sharon starts crying uncontrollably, and James takes her tighter into his arms and says, "It's all right, dear. I am trying to understand what you are going through. I am not mad with you. I was just trying to let you know that I know this is important to you. Please, dear, don't cry."

Sharon hugs James even tighter. And trying to calm down, she says, "I sure do love you. I don't know what I would do without you." Then looking at him, she tries to give him a little smile and a wet kiss on his cheek.

They stand embracing each other until Sharon has gained control of herself again. Then Sharon asks James, "Would you like something to eat now while it is still hot? I think that would do us both good. Then we can sit and talk. I will try to tell you about my trip. Is that okay with you, honey?"

James nods, so Sharon gets the food onto their plates. While James takes and gets some drinks ready, he has a feeling they will both need them tonight.

After dinner, they curl up in front of the fireplace, where James had built a nice fire. James looks at Sharon and says, "Are you sure you feel like talking tonight? I know I wanted to hear about your trip, but seeing you are still alive and after watching you during dinner, maybe we could get to know each other again and talk later."

Sharon is ready for that idea and moves closer to James, saying, "Are you sure about this, James?"

James replies, "Yes, I think both of us need a break from your House of Thoughts and do what comes naturally."

Sharon, now with a genuine smile on her face, says, "Boy, you sure know what I need and when I need it. I am so glad you are mine. Now let's get started. It has been too long already."

After their reunion, both James and Sharon take a hot shower and head for their nice, comfortable bed, where there will be no trips tonight. They can lie in each other's arms all night and wake together in the morning.

The alarm goes off, and their hands meet together on the button to turn it off. Sharon smiles at James and says, "Good morning, dear. Guess what? I am making coffee for you this morning." With that, she is out of bed and down the stairs into the kitchen. With coffee going, she heads to the front room and turns on the TV and thinks about the wonderful evening James and she had last night.

James walks into the front room to join her, and she looks up at him and says, "I just want to thank you for such a wonderful night and to let you know I really, really, really enjoyed myself. Do you think I repeated really enough in there for you to understand how much last night meant to me?"

James giggles and responds, "You are too kind to me, my dear. Couldn't you tell I was trying to please myself? Now if you received satisfaction in the process, well you could say we had a double blessing."

With that, they both laugh, and Sharon rises to kiss James good morning. "Would you like to be late for work this morning?" Sharon whispers laughingly in his ear, which makes them both laugh that much harder.

Finally, the laughter quiets down, and James looks at Sharon with love in his eyes and says, "My dear, last night was wonderful, and I knew we both needed that. But I would like to maybe go to the lake tonight and talk. You seem to enjoy the lake this time of year, and getting you out of this house and away from your thoughts would not hurt you a bit."

Sharon agrees with James, so they make plans to have dinner at the lake.

With James off to work and Sharon alone in the house again, she starts to get busy. *I know I will get the spring-cleaning done, which I have been meaning to do anyway. Maybe that will keep my mind occupied, and I will not have time to think about my last trip to the House of Thoughts.*

Then again, James is going to want to know why I am gone so long this last time. How do I tell him if I do not know myself? Maybe I need to figure out some of the mess that is in my head.

So much for spring-cleaning, and with that, Sharon heads for her study and sits down in front of her computer.

Here we go again.

2

The Big Question

Sharon arrives on the porch of the big old house in record time today. *The light is bright, and the air smells so wonderful,* she thinks. That is when Mrs. Thought comes to the door and invites Sharon in, but Sharon's response is, "Please, if you do not mind, would you ask Love to come outside? It is such a beautiful day. I would rather take a walk about the grounds, if that is satisfactory with you."

Mrs. Thought smiles one of her lovely smiles and retreats back into the house to call Love. Sharon seams rather relieved to be able to stay outside today. There is some sixth sense awake in her today, that does not want her entering the House of Thoughts, and she is not going to fight that feeling anymore.

"May we take a walk in the garden today, Love?" Sharon asks as Love appears at the door.

Love smiles at Sharon. "You are really getting good at following your senses, Sharon. I am so happy for you. You are going to find out things are going to start getting easier for you."

As they walk through the garden, Love is quiet and waits for Sharon to speak. Finally, Sharon says, "You know, Love, I have been doing a lot of thinking lately and have come to the conclusion that all of your thoughts have been with me since I was born. I am just coming to the knowledge of you as I begin to search around in my inner being.

"You said the other night that I had the answer to my question already and that after I got a good night's sleep, it would come to me. I am here to ask you if I am right. Do you remember the question?"

Love speaks and says, "You mean, 'How do you know whom to believe?'"

Sharon nods, and Love continues, "Yes, I remember."

Sharon then continues about what she has figured out. "When I awoke this morning, the answer just looked so clear. Now, if you will confirm for me that I am walking in truth and not leaning to my own understanding, I will be satisfied. Here goes: You first look inside yourself for Peace about what you are thinking and hearing. If you will let Peace, inner peace, be your guide, you will not go wrong."

Love stated, "It is written, 'All things are lawful, but not all things are profitable.' In another place, it is written, 'Try everything. Cling to that which is good and discard that which is does not work for you.'" Love looks at Sharon and smiles while she speaks. "If you look in *Webster* for Peace, you find 'freedom from anxiety, annoyance, or other mental disturbance.' I have to tell you, Sharon, that you now have the right answer."

Now Sharon is smiling from ear to ear as she hugs Love and says, "I just want to thank you for calling me to this wonderful place and waking me up to so many things. I know now that it was you who I heard calling me that first night. Now I would like to ask you one more question before I go home. I had a feeling there was a lot going on in the house when I first came and that if I had gone in, I was walking into a lot of confusion. Was I right?"

Love laughs and nods yes and says, "Before you go any further, let's just say it is nothing I cannot manage and leave it at that. Now you have a big night ahead of you, and I do not want any more in that mind of yours than what you need to have. I will see you when you come back, and I look forward to that, but for now, go get yourself ready for your night with James."

Sharon says, "I know I will be back, but for now I have to admit, you are right. I do have a big night coming. Goodbye for now."

With Peace as her guide, Sharon leaves.

3

The Lake

Sharon awakes at home with Peace growing inside her as she goes about getting ready for a wonderful night at the lake with James.

First, she thinks, *What should we have to eat? Maybe we could just stop and get something on the way.* Then she grabs a blanket and the cooler. *I will put some good drinks in the cooler because I know James will want to celebrate after we have our talk tonight. I know I am definitely ready. I felt like my mind was a jumbled up puzzle a few days ago. Now I can see an actual picture coming together.*

When James comes home, Sharon meets him at the door with an armful of things to take to the lake. She then asks James if he would not mind stopping at Paddy Shack for something to eat on the way out. James agrees, so they load up the truck and away they go. They do not know they head for a journey that is to become a turning point in their lives.

Sharon enjoys the talk with James during their drive to the lake about how his day has gone. He has had a good day at work and had accomplished a lot.

They end up stopping at Paddy Shack for dinner. After eating, James says, "I have noticed a different spirit about you today. When are you going to let me in on your new secret?"

Sharon just smiles and says, "As soon as we find a quiet place and get set up. There is so much I want to share with you, and I don't want any intrusions."

As they drive around the lake, they spot a place where nobody could come upon them by surprise. They both unload the truck, and Sharon lays out the blanket for them to sit on. James carries the cooler over to the blanket, looks inside, and declares, "Are we going to have a party or just sit here and get drunk?"

Sharon looks at him and laughs as she reaches for a drink. "Now, doesn't that all depend on you, my dear? I said earlier that I had a lot to share and did not want any interruptions. So grab a beer and listen, okay."

James reaches for a beer and asks, "Does this mean I can't say anything until you are done?"

Sharon shakes her head and explains, "Not exactly. I would like you to jump in if you have any questions, but the Lord willing, I will be able to answer many of your questions as I go. Now before we get started, I would like to thank you again for last night." Sharon reaches across the blanket to give James a big hug.

As Sharon sits back, she starts, "Now to begin, I know you already know some of what I have learned. Now I would like to bring you up to date, so to speak. The other night, when I was gone for so long, I want you to know I learned a lot from Love. Do you remember me talking about him? Anyway, you had asked me a question about how we could know whom to believe. I had to go ask Love, but when I got there, he had Experience and Understanding there for me to meet. Faith, Belief, and many others were there also. I know I am not making much sense yet, but just wait, I will get there.

"I have learned how our persuasion, faith, belief, trust, and confidence are all connected. Remember the saying from the Bible, which goes, 'The kingdom of God is as if a man should scatter seed on the ground.'" She then later explains what happens to the seed sown, which is first the blade, then the head, after that, the full grain in the head. "Now our persuasion comes from the word or seeds scattered by others, which we hear, planted in our heart, which in so many cultures is called faith. And then our belief is the blade, trust is the head, and confidence is the full grain in the head. In other terminology, our belief is the first thing we see of a word that is planted in our hearts. You cannot have a flower until you plant a seed. You know you cannot believe in something until you know or hear that it exists. Then our trust starts to grow as we believe in that word, and then our confidence is the part we harvest and keep to build bigger crops. When we plant faith and let it grow to full term, that is when we can say we have a crop of confidence."

James looks at Sharon and starts to speak, but Sharon hurries to continue and says, "I know I haven't answered your question yet, but I am getting there. Like I said, Experience was there, and I had a chance to get a word from him. He said he was what carried us through life. Depending on our experiences, we get understanding. What I mean is knowing whether something work for us or not. Either we can guide him with our faith or if we are not strong in our faith, others could take the reins with their faith. When we let others lead with their faith, that is when things in our life might get bumpy.

"The way to know whom you should listen to is by the amount of Peace that comes from the words others speak to you or by trying their ideas out and experiencing things for yourself. I have found out that when Peace is not around that seed of faith, you learn you do not have a good seed but know you have a weed. You have heard of the fruit of the Spirit. Peace is one of those fruits. Also, there is joy, which is just as good. Joy, I have found out, is where we draw on strength from to control our experiences. Remember the saying 'The joy of the Lord is our strength'? Well, if you realize, words are what we use to live our lives and know they are our Lord. Now, finding out our Lord God has the best words to live by, you could then say the joy of God's words is our strength."

Sharon finally sits quiet and waits for James to speak. Hope builds inside her that James receives the right message from her words. From the look on his face, Sharon can tell that James is trying to sort out all the information. She just has to give him some time and space; she has said all she can for the time being.

Finally, after what seems hours to Sharon, James speaks. "Wow! That makes a lot of sense to me now that you put it that way. I mean, no wonder you were gone so long the other night. Sounds likes you had a lot on your plate to figure out. You know, Sharon, you make it sound like words are especially important to the way we live. Now just not any words, but God's words are the best word to hear. If others do not agree with God's words, then you will know not to listen to them."

Sharon starts to smile and grabs James around the neck and rolls him over on the ground. "Me thinks you've got it, old chap. Can we celebrate now?" Sharon asks, and then she kisses James to start the celebration.

They kiss each other as childhood sweethearts, oblivious to the outside world. Just as things are really getting hot, James remembers they are still at the lake and, gently pulling back from Sharon, softly says, "I love you so very much, but I think we could get into a lot of trouble if we don't stop and take control of ourselves until we get home, my dear." As he sits up, he asks, "Now, would you like a fresh cold drink to cool yourself off?"

Sharon realizes things are getting a little out of hand and sits up herself. Smoothing out her hair, she responds, "I think that sounds like a marvelous idea, but you just wait until I get you home."

Laughing, she takes a fresh drink from James, and holding it up, she makes a toast. "Here's to the best husband a woman could ever have. I want to thank you, dear, for standing beside me through all this. I also want you to know, I thank God for giving you to me."

James holds up his drink and says, "Here's to us, kid. I think, when God put us together, He made us a good team."

As they click their cans, they both say, "From the top to the bottom and all the way through the middle together. For we are in it to win it, and we are winning. In Jesus's name, amen." They both take a drink and go on to enjoy a wonderful evening at the lake together.

On the way home, Sharon looks at James and says, "Thank you for a wonderful evening. I have not felt this relaxed in days. I am looking forward to starting a new way of life with you. I wonder what the kids will say to my latest information. Do you think I should tell them right away, or should we try this system first?"

James responds, "Us first. But let's talk about all that tomorrow, dear. It is late, and I want to finish at home what we started at the lake."

Sharon smiles and agrees with him, but she knows she will have to talk to Melody and the boys soon. Sharon knows her and James are growing closer, and soon they will be as one.

4

Children's Turn

After a good night's sleep and with James off to work, Sharon decides to go see Melody, her oldest child and only daughter. You see, this mother-and-daughter team are remarkably close, always talking and sharing their lives more than other mothers and daughters that they know. She thinks, with Melody on her side, Wyatt, Steven, and Joel, who are her sons, will have to hear with the three speaking the same thing. Sharon is finding out there is strength in numbers. Not to say the boys are hard, but she knows they are not easy either.

After her talk with Melody, she realizes that none of this is going to be as easy as she first thought. The more she tries to explain where she has been and all the things she has learned there, the more Melody seams to look at her with confusion.

Then Wisdom shows up, saying, "One step at a time, Sharon. Remember the saying 'Precept upon precept, and line upon line. A little here and a little there, which is the way to get this job done.' Therefore, instead of telling them everything at once and having them think you have gone crazy, you need to become an example for them. Teaching them what you learn by doing and applying the innovative words to your own life. And if they ask, then tell them."

Sharon agrees with Wisdom totally, and soon she is thinking on how she can apply her latest information to her life. She feels that is her mission in this life, which is to be an example for others to follow so they can find peace of mind in their hearts, along with realizing Love is the best leader to follow.

Sharon turns back to Melody and says, "I realize this is a lot for you to take all at once. Please take a moment to think back and look at the changes which have happened in your mother's life in just the last few weeks."

Melody takes a second and then says, "Well, you are not sick anymore, and you are even driving again. Matter of fact, now that you mention it, you seem to be more confident of yourself than I ever remember. Mom, I need to let you know, from my point of view, this just seems like a lot to swallow all at one time."

Sharon takes Melody in her arms. "I agree with you, my dear. I had a hard time at first myself. I promise I will give you time to adjust your mind to all this news, but I just had to share with you why I am doing so much better. All I am really asking from you is watch and learn. Then help me convey the message to your brothers, okay?"

Melody looks up at her mother and answers, "I will try my best."

"That is all I ask of you, Mel, and I know your best will work just fine," Sharon says.

The following weekend, Joel is coming back into town, so all the kids ask to meet at Steven's house for a get-together, and plans are made. James and Sharon decide to talk with the kids. James will take the boys and Sharon the girls.

When James and Sharon get to Steven's, Melody and Wyatt are already there as usual, waiting on Joel. After hugs and kisses all around, they see Joel finally pulling in the drive. More hugs and kisses make the rounds, and then everyone heads to the backyard.

Steven and Joel start up the grill, and Steven's wife, Amber, with Melody and Sharon start setting the table. James and Wyatt, with Melody's husband, Caleb, start setting up the targets to throw darts, which everybody enjoys playing.

The weather is on its best behavior, and the conversations are readily accepted by male and female. Sharon figures Melody has thought about what Mom had said and shared with her brothers a lot more than Sharon has expected. Things go so smoothly that when James and Sharon leave, they can only thank Love for leading them and intervening.

In Charge

Once I wondered who's in charge
Because my problems were so large
On days when upon myself I did rely
Nothing worked, no matter what I try

Then this voice popped into my head
Why not try trusting in Me instead?
I know just what you're going through
I know the reason that you are blue

I have the solutions, so just ask
I have the solutions to any task
I have put my solutions in a book
Now for a solution, just take a look

Look in your Bible for what I said
Take my words, and fill your head
Preparing the mind belongs to man
Answer of the tongue is in MY HAND

My Word is precious, more than gold
Use My Word, and become very bold
Don't tackle those problems all alone
Rely on My Word, and become strong

So speak in My hearing I'll do for you
The choice is yours to be happy or blue
Now bless or curse, you make the choice
It's from the abundance I give voice

PART 6

Time to Move On
Let Us Come Together

1

Brand-New Day

Sharon and James keep growing closer. They increasingly begin enjoying their new lives as they learn more of God's words and start applying them to their lives. Melody and the boys start noticing the difference in Mom and Dad, and so James keeps filling them in about each awesome new thing that Sharon has learned. Little by little, they are all starting to work together.

Grace comes and rests with Sharon, and she goes on to author a book called "Words." This book helps her share the truths she has found and her experiences with her family. Little does Sharon know just how much there is left to learn.

She continues to study about where words come from and how they get here. Little by little, she grows, a little here and a little there. Her trips to the House of Thoughts are becoming increasingly often. Sharon is becoming obsessed with all the joy she receives from the thoughts she is learning. Then she enjoys trying to put an order to all her innovative words.

Then one day it happens. While sorting some of her new thoughts, she hears Love call to her from the house. She can tell his voice anywhere now, so off she goes back to the House of Thoughts, but today will be incredibly special for her.

As Sharon arrives, she notices something new. Why she never saw this before totally escapes her. She calls out quickly to Love and says, "Love, look, there is more to this old house, a lot more than what I have been seeing, isn't there? I never realized that there was even an upstairs to this place, and now today, as I look, there could be possibly three extra floors up there." Sharon turns and looks Love straight in his eyes and continues, "May I ask, what kind of thoughts are you keeping from me?"

Now Love just smiles and says, "Yes. Well, it looks like you are ready to move up some more in your consciousness of thoughts and their life. I could not tell you about everything all at once. We have found, the best way to manage this situation is to let people grow at their own pace. We Thoughts are just here to guide, not control people's every move.

"The Creator gave the freedom to humanity to choose his own path. Just like you, when you met Lust and his group, you could have stayed there, kept listening to their voices, and died. You choose to hear my voice and come to me. Do you see the difference? By allowing people to grow on their own, nobody feels like they are being pushed into believing something they are not ready for and then later refusing it because it was not their thought after all."

Sharon is shaking her head as Love is speaking, but Love can tell she is only half listening, and finally Sharon says, "You know what, that makes a lot of sense to me now. Is it all right if I go exploring some more of this old house now?"

Love just looks at Sharon and nods yes but then says, "I would like for you to take some special thoughts with you while you go. This is totally unfamiliar territory for you, and I will not have anything happening to you. May I call Help and Grace?"

Sharon nods an okay, but her mind is already leaving without Help by her side. They will just have to catch up with her. She can barely hear Love yelling at her to wait in the background. Once again, Excitement has gotten a hold of her. She wants to find the stairs that will lead her up to the other floors of this big house. This time, Excitement leads her right to the first door of her new journey.

She opens the door and starts to enter but stops cold, for right there in front of her is the image of her mother. Immediately, Unbelief shows up, trying to grab a hold of her. She starts to slam the door shut, but Help and Strength arrive, and Sharon receives both of them and finds courage to speak up and find out for herself if what she is seeing is real or not.

Sharon, shaking her head, speaks softly, "Mother, is that really you?"

Her mother, whose name was Dorothy, nods a yes.

Now Sharon, with all her good friends, reaches out and touches the image of her mother. "You sure feel real. And now that I am this close, you even smell good, just like my mom." Then so many questions start coming out of Sharon's mouth. "What are you doing here? How did you get here? How long have you been here?"

Dorothy smiles and says, "Calm down a minute, my dear. Come, let's take a walk, and I will try and answer some of your questions." With that, Dorothy takes Sharon's arm and leads her out a back door of the house and onto a big porch.

As they walk arm in arm, Sharon feels Peace, Joy, Warmth, and of course Love join them. When they get outside, Sharon notices that everything happens to be twice as nice today. The words keep going through her brain: I am here with Mom. I am here with my mom.

Dorothy leads Sharon over to a table and chairs, which set out back of the old house, and motions for her to sit down. "I am so glad to see you, and I know you have a lot of questions going around that pretty little head of yours. First, let me look at you. While I look, you may at the same time take time to sort your questions and put them into perspective."

Love moves over, stands before Sharon, and asks, "Is it all right with you if I and the others stay, or would you rather have this first meeting with your mother alone?"

Sharon simply replies, "Love, you are the one that called me here in the first place, and you have shown me so many wonderful things here. I would consider it an honor if you would stay with us and remain part of our talk."

Dorothy begins by taking Sharon's hand and saying, "You look so good, my dear, and I am so happy to see you have made it this far. I always knew you would come. I can tell by the expression on your face that you know I am real, but you are still wondering why it took you so long to see me. The easiest way for me to put this is, I am a thought, like any other thought, and I am as real as any thought can be. I am just a little brighter and bigger than some other thoughts. Let me give you an example.

"Remember when you first get up in the morning and that light first comes on? The first reaction is to cover your eyes and peek out little by little, until your eyes adjust to that bright light. Then you are ready to face the day.

"Well, thoughts have light in them, some more than others, which make them become visible to the mind. Mrs. Thought and Love here knew what you could tolerate, and they helped you to get your mind's eye adjusted to the many thoughts that people must go through before they can come to this point."

Sharon looks at her mother and asks, "Am I dead now? Is that why I have made it this far?"

Love speaks quickly, "No, definitely not. You are just one of those special people that have done your study and are able to move on. You have always known your mother was here, but until now, your mind was not ready to accept that thought. I want to tell you I am so pleased to have watched you grow and advance to this point."

Sharon looks at her mother and says, "The thoughts, which stay up here, I have this feeling they are different rank than those downstairs. Your thoughts up here are written in a different book, right?"

Dorothy smiles and replies, "I can honestly say you've got it, though Webster does speak of us briefly. Webster calls us up here nouns, proper nouns, or *names*, which is just a way of saying we are entities which exist, not normally preceded by an article or other limiting modifier. We, as names, are written in an incredibly special book called the Lamb's Book of Life."

"Wow!" Sharon says and then carries on with, "I just started studying the different classes of words. Is that why I was called to move up?"

Dorothy and Love nod their heads yes.

"Well, now I know I am on the right track. I think I just found out that I have a lot more to study. Mom, I do not want to leave you so soon, but I have learned one thing about coming here, even if it were the hard way, which is, I do not stay too long at a time, or I would never want to leave. I can tell you this though: I will be back to see you soon," Sharon says as she stands, holding out her arms to give goodbye hugs.

Dorothy stands also to give her daughter a big hug, telling her she totally understands where she is coming from and that she is looking forward to their next visit. "Maybe next time you come, we can have your dad come and meet with you also. For now, I send my blessing and my best thoughts with you. Use all you want, and do not worry, they know to whom they belong. I will see you soon."

With goodbyes said and hugs given, Sharon leaves the House of Thoughts with lots of wonderful thoughts following her and proceeds to wake up in her office.

Sharon looks at the clock in her study and realizes she had been gone just a brief time this trip, but oh, how she had enjoyed herself. She is full of questions and energy. She decides to write down a few things while they are still fresh on her mind.

Let me see here, she thinks as she grabs her pen and paper. *I want to continue to find out more about the different classes of words, and the best way I know is to go to the book of words and see what Webster has written there. First, let me start with what I know and then go from there. Nouns, verbs, adjectives, and adverbs—these are the main classes of what I remember from school. After talking with Mom today, I think there is many groups of the word classes. I mean, there must be different ranks that go with each group. I remember something about the baby book of names, and each name has a different meaning. I think I will try to find one of those books.*

Then Sharon does a search and finds the form classes, also known as content words or open classes, include Nouns, Verbs, Adjectives, Adverbs.

The structure classes, also known as function words or closed classes, include Determiners, Pronouns, Auxiliaries, Conjunctions, Qualifiers, Interrogatives, Prepositions, Expletives, Particles.

Wow, Sharon thinks.

Just then, Sharon hears James coming down the stairs. She looks at her clock again and realizes that she has lost another night of sleeping with James. *Wow, is it already time to get James ready and off to work?* With this consideration, she looks back at her paper and says softly, "I'll get back to you after I get James off to work."

Sharon leaves her study and greets James at the bottom of the stairs, "Good morning, dear. Did you sleep well last night?"

James wrenches a smile onto his face. "I guess all right for a man that had to sleep alone. I sure did miss you last night. Did you enjoy another trip to the House of Thoughts? You know, dear, I really do not mind you going, but I sure wish you could get your timing down and be with me while I am home."

Guilt hits Sharon and she thinks it best not to tell James about running into Mom and having a talk with her, at least not yet. Sharon nods a quiet yes and then says, "I am sorry, honey, but I wasn't gone all night this time. It's just that when I got back, I felt I needed to take down some notes about what I had learned from Love before I forgot. I tell you what, let's go and have some coffee and watch the news together."

Then James sees that smile and the twinkle in her eyes. He knows he just cannot stay upset with that woman of his, no matter how hard he tries. Deciding to enjoy what time he can with her, he agrees and heads to the kitchen to start the coffee.

When James brings the coffee into the living room, he sets down their cups, takes Sharon's hand, and says, "Why don't we go out for dinner tonight and then catch a movie? I honestly feel you are spending too much time at that house, and I could sure use your company for a change."

Sharon starts to object, but the look in his eyes tells her he needs to have some time with her again. "I tell you what, I will try and get some notes down today and get a nap. Lord willing, I will be ready to go when you get home."

James smiles and takes Sharon in his arms and says, "Well, if that is the best you have to offer, then I'll take it and pray, God's will be done. Lord, please be willing that Sharon gets everything done. By the way, what did you find out last night that's got you so stirred up?"

Sharon leans back and looks at James to see if he can tell how deep she has gone into the House of Thoughts. After deciding that he just wants to be involved in her life, she says, "The best way to put this is, I learned I have a lot of studying to do about nouns and verbs."

James gives her that ugh look, so she continues, "I will tell you later. But for now, I want to let you know, I do appreciate all the time you have sacrificed for me. Honey, give me a big kiss, and let's make plans for tonight."

With their plans for this evening made and James dressed, he finally leaves for work. Sharon heads to her study and starts back on her list of nouns and verbs. She looks at *Webster* but decides the print is too small for her tired eyes. Therefore, she opens her Encarta Encyclopedia and looks up nouns. Her search takes her to the section marked "Parts of Speech." *Delightful book*, she thinks as she realizes everything she needs is right here. *Wow!* She thinks when she reads that the word *noun* came from the Latin word *nomen*, meaning *name*.

Sharon gets a lot of information written down and then decides that if her and James were going out for the evening, she should take a nap so she would be ready when he gets home. She is actually starting to look forward to getting out of the house and spending time with him.

The plans they have made sound fun. They are going to Applebee's for dinner, and then they are going to see that new show that everybody is talking about, *The Passion of the Christ*. She has heard the movie has extreme violence in it but still a must-see picture. *I guess I will find out for myself tonight*, she thinks as she heads for the shower. After a hot shower, she is definitely ready to head upstairs to get some sleep.

2

Old Habits

Now anyone knows the fact that it takes three weeks to create a new habit, which helps replace an old habit.

With that said, let us get back to Sharon, shall we?

Sharon crawls into bed with thoughts of the coming night on her mind. But as she drifts off to sleep, she remembers being with her mother just hours before. Her mother had passed on ten years ago, and many times Sharon had wished she could talk with her mom again. Many things had happened in her life, which she wants to let her mom know about. For example, she now has fourteen grand-children, and Melody has number 15 in the oven, so to speak. These thoughts keep coming into her mind, and next thing she knows, she finds herself back at the House of Thoughts.

This time, she already knows her way to the door that leads up the stairs to where her mom is. As Sharon approaches the back of the house, she can see her mom standing there, waiting for her. "I can't sneak up on you at all, can I?" Sharon calls to her mom.

With a warm smile, her mother calls back, "No, but I don't mind you trying. There are a lot of thoughts around here that let me know when you are coming and what is on your mind."

"You mean there are no surprises here?" Sharon asks her mom. "That sounds very boring, if you ask me."

"Oh, Surprise is here. But when it comes to you, well let's just say, I have the word out that you are kind of special to me, and I like knowing about you," her mom replies.

"Then you already know about the grandbabies and everything I wanted to tell you?" Sharon looks a little upset as she speaks.

Dorothy lovingly takes her daughter in her arms and whispers, "Melody is going to have a little girl, and she will call her Haley Rena. She will grow up and be a fine young woman. She will be an important leader someday. Would you like to know anything else?" There is a short pause as Dorothy looks and sees tears begin to come to her daughter's eyes. Then she continues, "I might not have shown you just how special you are to me while I was with you on earth, but I want you to know now."

Boy, oh, boy, this news totally takes her by surprise. Sharon just starts crying. And let me tell you, the tears really flows. Yes, she knows that her mom and she were close, but this is more than she has ever dared to imagine.

Dorothy holds her daughter close until the tears subside. When Sharon is finally calm again, Dorothy tells her, "Sharon, I love you very much, and I am going to keep an ear open so I can learn all I can about your life. For now, my dear, I also know you and James have a wonderful night planned. Now you need to get home and get that beauty sleep. Oh, by the way, I also wanted to mention that you are on the right track with your studies. Love you, dear, and I will see you soon." Dorothy kisses Sharon goodbye and sends her daughter back home.

As Sharon leaves, she hears one last thought from her mom.

"Oh, by the way, Sharon, bring your other half in on your studies. Two heads are better than one. James is a lot tougher than you give him credit for. Remember the saying you two say every day. Listen to your mother please."

Sharon wakes in her bed with wonderful thoughts about what to wear for her date tonight with James. After becoming completely awake, she realizes she had been to see her mother. She finds a great deal of Peace had accompanied her home. Sharon, in her mind, finally speaks to Worry and lets him know, loud and clear, "Worry, you have no more room in my thoughts. Now I know for sure, Mom is on top of everything."

One more thought quickly passes in her mind. "I am sure looking forward to being with her someday, but for now, as Mom put it, I have a wonderful night ahead of me, and I need to get ready." With that said and done, she opens her closet and picks out the blue dress, which she knows is James's favorite, and starts to get ready.

Just as Sharon finishes, she hears James pull in the drive. Earlier she had not known whether to let James know about seeing Mom, but now she is sure it is time to bring the two of them together, to work all these thoughts through. First, a wonderful evening, and then she will talk with him.

James, tonight I am totally yours, she thinks. *I am here to please you and to let Love bring us even closer together.*

James comes in the back door, tired and dirty, for it had been a grueling day at work. He takes one look at Sharon, and a smile comes to his face. "I sure was hoping, after such a rough day, you would be ready to go. I can tell you now, Fear sure was trying hard to get his grip on me by saying, your studies were more important to you than I could ever be. Now that Fear sees you standing there, all dressed up and ready to go, he just had to leave. There was nothing else he could say."

Sharon goes into James's arms and gives him a big hug and kiss then, backing off, says, "By the way, my dear, I hope you never forget this message as I am going to say it loud and clear. I want you to know, beyond any doubt, that you are especially important to me. I would like to ask you if you would like to come deeper into my study with me. If so, then we can talk about the matter over dinner. But for now, if we are going to make the show on time, I think you need to start getting ready."

James then heads off to be showered and dressed.

3

A Night to Remember

James showers and dresses in record time. Therefore, when they get to the restaurant, they end up with plenty of time to enjoy their meal and have that talk Sharon wants to have. Sharon finds James eager to hear about her new adventure to the House of Thoughts. He seems to get excited when she tells him about finding out there is more to that old house than what she first thought. Then she explains she actually had a meeting with her mother.

When she gets into the part about different ranks or classes to words, James jumps in and says, "Well, my time in the service may help us out in that area. Maybe I can take some time tonight and write down all the ranks of the military I remember." He looks at Sharon and sees a puzzled look on her face, so he asks, "Do you think that will help you?"

Sharon smiles and says, "You just keep amazing me. Earlier today, I had Worry telling me you would get upset with me if I told you just how deep I had gone. Now I look at you sitting here, more eager than I could imagine, ready to jump in with both feet, no hesitation at all. All I can say is wow!" I can tell you now, I was not going to say anything yet, but when I went back and talked to Mom again, she told me not to let Worry have his way and to go ahead and bring you into this matter. Now for an answer to your question, I think you are definitely on the right track."

James takes her hand, smiles, and looks her straight in the eyes. "My dear, it sounds like you had a time with Worry, while I had Fear working on me. I want to let you know here and now, I love you, and I am looking forward to finding out the ranks of words and just where we stand in that ranking. I also agree with your mom when she said we are stronger standing together."

Sharon stands and goes to James, and they embrace.

Finally, James says, "Now, shall we pay our bill and go see this controversial show and find out what all this uproar is about?"

James and Sharon enter the theater, just as others are coming out. They notice, on their way through the crowd, that some are crying, saying the movie is great, while others say the movie is excessively violent. They enter the show saying to each other, "I guess we will have to watch and judge for ourselves."

After the movie, they walk out of the theater without saying a word. They also ride home in silence. But when they enter the house, James turns to Sharon and says, "Did you see the way they beat him? Then they had him carry that big cross all the way through town. Boy, I feel like such a failure. I complain I am tired after working eight hours. I cannot imagine working that long and then walking that far, carrying that big cross, let alone taking a beating like that first. That would definitely be a lot worse than just working."

Sharon, with tears still seeping from her eyes, looks at James and says, "We are all in the same boat. That is why He came and did the job we could not do."

James tries to interrupt by saying something about how he should be able to be stronger, but Sharon holds up her hand to stop him and continues, "James, while watching them crucify the man called Jesus, I saw past the flesh. I saw Love himself up there on that cross. Oh, James, I knew there was something special about Love when I first went to the House of Thoughts and met him, but I could not put my finger on it until tonight. Remember how it is written, 'In your weakness He is made strong.'"

James takes Sharon into his arms and tries to comfort her, but she pulls away and starts her pacing back and forth. James, after being married to her for all these years, knows what that means, so he just sits down and waits for her to figure things out in her head.

Finally, she crosses the floor, sits down next to him, and says, "Thank you for knowing me and loving me. I feel a lot better now. I would like to explain my outburst if you are ready."

James nods yes, so Sharon continues, "You see, Love was the first resident Mrs. Thought introduced me to. I had a strange feeling, even back then, that I knew him but could not remember if we had ever met. Then tonight, as I watched that movie, the voice as the actor talked kept sounding familiar. Then when I saw them crucify him, that is when I saw Love show his face. That is when I knew I know this man. I have read and heard about Love my whole life. Do you see where I am coming from?" Sharon stares at him, desperate to have James understand.

"Are you saying the word *love* itself was inside the man we call Jesus?" James responds with surprise in his voice.

"Yes, that is exactly what I am saying. The word *thought* and all the meaning of love was there for the universe to see." Sharon sighs a sigh of relief and leans back in the chair.

Then it is James's turn to stand and take the floor. He starts with, "Well, if that be the case, then it is imperative for us to figure out our own standing in the word classes and to get busy doing what we were meant to do." With that said, James starts to grab a pen and paper to write down the ranks he knows from his time in the service.

Sharon reaches over and gently takes his arm and says, "I am sorry if I got you all fired up. I know it is late, and you have people coming in the morning. I just had a reality hit me tonight. I guess you could say I let that reality carry me away. We both know we have come a long way. We also know we have a long way to go. But trying to push ahead when we are tired and emotional can lead to mistakes."

"So with that said, may I make a suggestion? I say we get a good night's sleep and start fresh tomorrow. Then when we have time, we can put the pieces together slowly and see how they fit."

James lays down his paper and looks at his wife with new insight to her inner being. "You sure are getting smart in your old age."

Sharon reaches up and pops him on the arm as they both start laughing. "You have to admit though, I am moving better now since I have learned from God's word in number 14 about as we speak in His hearing that is what he will do for us. Now, old man, would you like to go upstairs and cuddle for a while before we drift off to sleep?"

James grabs Sharon laughingly, and off they go to bed, with both of their minds on the same thing.

4

Together

As James and Sharon fall asleep that night, they are both thinking it is time for them to pull our thoughts together and start working as one. Soon they will know just how close they are to achieving their saying, which goes like this: "From the top to the bottom and all the way through the middle together." Wrapped in each other's arms, they drift off into a very deep sleep.

Then it happens. James opens his eyes and sees a wonderful place. At first, he thinks this place sure does look familiar. And then he thinks, *I must be dreaming because this place looks just like the place Sharon describes as her place.*

Then he hears a voice behind him saying, "Well, are you just going to stand there?"

As he turns around, there is Sharon standing there, looking at him with a big smile on her face.

"Am I dreaming about your place, or have we actually made the trip together?" James says with a little hesitation in his voice.

Sharon takes James calmly by the hand and tries to explain what she thinks has happened. "Well, I think, between what we have said for years and what Mom said about bringing you into my study, well, looks like it has now come to pass. I knew we were to get closer, but

I did not think this far. But I sure am glad you made the journey. James, may I have the honor of showing you around this wonderful place? Then I would like to take you up to the House of Thoughts and introduce you to some wonderful thoughts."

James slowly looks around and then back at Sharon. "You know, dear, this place is just as lovely as you described. I think I would really enjoy you showing me around, but I do not think I am ready to meet too many thoughts just yet. You realize this is my first trip, and I am not quite sure how things go here."

Sharon can see Worry trying to grab James from behind, so she says, "James, trust me. I know this is your first time. I will let you go at your own pace. Would you like to meet Love and let him go with us?"

Before James can answer, they hear a voice, "Did I hear my name mentioned?"

They both look around and find Love standing there, reaching his hand toward James, and saying, "I am so glad to finally see you face-to-face. It would be a great honor if you would let me stroll around the grounds with you two."

James is instantly at ease with Love, so at ease that while looking in the face of Love, James just blurts out, "Wow, it was you up there on that cross. I just have to ask why. I mean, how could you take all that pain and still forgive us?"

Love just simply says, "My Father sent me to fulfill what he said I would do, so that is what I did. I do not want to get too far ahead of myself, so I will tell you, you will learn more about My Father later. For now, how would you like to take a tour of the lands?"

James agrees a walk around the grounds sounds wonderful. The day is beautiful, with the sun shining so bright. As they walk along, James mentions that he feels everything here seems so much more alive, way more than he remembers in the other world. Sharon just has to giggle, for that is the same thing she had thought when she first arrived.

What seems like such a brief time to James, Love is saying, "Soon it will be time for you to go. You can only stay so long at the House of Thoughts. The attraction to this place can become overwhelming if you are not prepared and stay too long." Just that fast, he is then saying, "I hope you enjoyed your tour and look forward to seeing you again soon."

Sharon does not at first see what is happening; she just says her goodbye to Love and takes James by the hand and leaves. Then she turns, looks him in the eyes, and says, "Time to wake up, James. Hey, James, the alarm is going off. Would you reach up and shut that thing off please? James, wake up!" Sharon yells as she shakes him into consciousness, but it is just like pulling teeth. Sharon then realizes she has to bring James back to this side of life.

James moans and groans a little but finally wakes, enough to realize he is in his bed with Sharon; the alarm is going off; and he has a customer coming over in a little while. Slowly he reaches up, shuts off the alarm, and looking at his wife, he says, "Wow, did I have a wonderful dream or what?"

Sharon pats him on the arm and says, "Yes, you most definitely did, my dear, if that is what you want to call the trip we took."

This brings James to full awareness. "You mean that was all real, and I really got to meet Love?"

Sharon nods her head and kisses James on the cheek, then rolls over to get out of bed. "I will see you downstairs, my dear. And if you have any questions, I will try and answer what I can."

As Sharon tries to get out of bed, James quickly grabs her by her arm, pulls her closer, and states, "I have only one question. That is, 'Why couldn't I stay? That place was so beautiful and peaceful. I just do not understand why we had to come back to this place."

"Get dressed and meet me downstairs. I will try to explain the reason then, but I think you already know why. Take your time and think about it," Sharon says gently as she pulls herself away.

As James is coming down the stairs, there is a knock at the door. *Good*, Sharon thinks. *That must be Keith, James's costumer.* James gives Sharon that look she knows so well that says, "We will talk later." And with that, he answers the door and heads outside to deal with the matters at hand. Sharon just says a small prayer, "Lord, please let Keith be his normal self, and keep him busy so I can have some time to figure out some things. Thank you."

5

Get Things Right

As Sharon enters her study, she realizes that many of James's thoughts are coming with her. She shuts the door behind her and goes over to her desk. There she sits down and speaks aloud, "Love, I need to speak with you please, the sooner the better. And could you please bring Wisdom, Understanding, and Help with you? The rest of you thoughts, I am asking, please…I need for you to leave." Then she proceeds to sit down, wait for everybody else to leave, and Love, with his group, to show up.

Sharon is soon back at the house of thought, and Love has everyone waiting for her. She looks at Love and asks what just happened. Love takes Sharon by the arm and gently leads her a little way from the group.

"I know that James wanted to stay, but it is not his time to come here permanently. Let me explain it to you this way. I called you because you were looking for the truth, which is why you are not in any danger of staying too long.

"You are like our messenger for those around you on the other side. You need to explain to James that for right now, he is only to receive the truth and help you help others. Let him know it will be a while before either of you come here to stay. If he will have a help-ing-others attitude, there will not be any problems."

Sharon has a few more questions she needs answers to, and she figures that since James will be tied up with Keith for quite a while, this will be a good opportunity.

Sharon proceeds to have a long talk with Love and asks Wisdom and Understanding to become involved in Love's answers.

"Time sure does fly when you are having fun." This is what James used to wake up Sharon with after her naps. Sharon realizes James has come into her study and is speaking to her. "Looks like you are trying to catch up on the sleep you lost last night. Would you like to go up and take a nap with me? That sure does sound good to me if you are willing."

"That sounds good to me also," Sharon responds quickly, trying to hide the fact that she has not really been asleep at all.

Then she remembers what Love had told her, and she quickly says, "First, we need to have a small talk. Did you get Keith taken care of?"

James nods, and Sharon continues, "Remember when you woke up this morning and wanted some answers? Well, I went and had a talk with Love, and he told me we need to talk before you go back."

James looks at her with a little bit of surprise and with a hurt look in his eyes. "Did I do something wrong? Am I not allowed back there anymore?"

Sharon smiles, takes him by the hand, and motions for him to sit as she shakes her head no. After he has taken a seat next to her, she states, "You did nothing wrong at all, my dear. I was the one at fault. I wanted you with me so much. I forgot to prepare you in the right way. That is why I need to talk with you now."

James replies, "I do not understand what you mean 'your fault.'"

Sharon holds up her hand and continues, "You see, I know that place is real, and your first instinct is to want to stay, but you and I are on a mission of sorts. We are there to learn the truth and bring that truth back to our friends and family. I can tell you this: I am going to need your help because there is still a lot to learn before we can go there and stay for good."

"Are you saying, that is the place where we will be forever after we are done with our jobs here on this side?" James responds with joy in his voice.

Sharon nods a yes as the thought hits them both at the same time.

"That sure is more than I imagined."

With smiles on both their faces, Sharon says, "Now I think we are diffidently ready for that nap."

They head up the stairs arm in arm with Peace all around them, now knowing they were in this thing together.

As they reach the bed, James says, "May I ask you a question, my dear?"

Sharon nods, so James continues, "Who do you think we will meet next?"

"Let's just wait and see. But I can let you know, most definitely, Love will be with us all the way through our learning process."

With that, they kiss each other and fall asleep.

6

Going Slow

Since you readers already know, I will not disappoint you. James and Sharon again head together to the other side. This time, Mr. Think is there to greet them. After the introductions to Mr. Think, Sharon takes James up the path to the House of Thoughts.

As they approach the big house, James says, "Wow, Sharon, you were not kidding about the size of this house. I have to tell you, until now I just could not imagine a house this big."

Sharon just smiles and says, "Just wait, James." Then looking up on the porch, she says, "Oh, James, there is Mrs. Thought."

There, standing on the porch, is Mrs. Thought. She is reaching out her hand to greet James as they come up to the door. Then she says, "Welcome, James. So glad to see you have made the journey with our beloved Sharon. I can tell she has filled you in on a lot of the information about us here. I just wanted to meet you face-to-face and let you know Love is waiting for you two in his room. He asked me not to let the other thoughts get you confused. So if you will please follow me, I will show you the way."

Mrs. Thought leads them through a passageway so not to disturb the other residents who are in the parlor. When they reach Love's door, Mrs. Thought turns to leave but then turns back and gives James a big hug. "I am so glad you have made the trip. Sharon looks much more complete with you. You both belong together, and it does my heart good to see this come to past." Then she bids them both adios and leaves.

As they watch Mrs. Thought leave, James and Sharon hear a voice from within, "Come on in, my children. I have so much to tell you, so let us get started."

James turns back around, opens the door to Love's room, and enters, with Sharon following remarkably close.

Truth is sitting there with Love, and James functions as if he knows this is the way things are to be. There, standing in a robe, which looks as if it has blood all over it, is Love.

Love crosses the room and speaks to James, "I can tell the thoughts I sent to you this afternoon did their job."

Then, turning to Sharon, Love says, "Excuse me, dear, let me fill you in. I heard the talk you had with James before you both went to sleep this afternoon. Therefore, I sent Wisdom, Peace, and Understanding to talk with him before you two left for your trip. Don't you think they did a wonderful job?"

Sharon looks at James and sees the Peace that's shown from his face. Then she finally realizes why James is not asking questions. Everything becomes truly clear to Sharon. At that moment, she knows that James is the one needed here to complete the mission that she was called only to start. Sharon walks over to James and willingly takes her place next to her husband, and right then they become one flesh.

James turns, kisses, and receives Sharon into himself. From that moment, he knows he will never be without her again. He then calmly turns to Love and says, "I am now ready to learn Truth and go as I am sent and to show that Truth to the world."

The meeting now begins with Love taking the floor and introducing Truth to James. Then Love informs James, "The first thing we want you to make known to the world is the story of Un."

PART 7

The Truth about Un

1

New Leader

Sharon wakes up in bed and proceeds to go downstairs to prepare dinner. She knows James will be ready to eat when he gets back. Then there will be a lot of discussion about the best way to get started.

Now, dear readers, I hope you do not think I will do away with one of the main characters.

James comes down the stairs about three hours later. The glow around him has increased greatly, and Sharon goes to him and says, "I am so glad you have taken your position as the head of this mission. With Love guiding you and you guiding me, now I know we cannot go wrong. I fixed fried chicken and dressing for dinner. Let us eat. And then, if you feel up to it, we will talk."

"Sounds like you were reading my mind there, dear," James says with a smile. They both start laughing and head off to enjoy a delicious meal together.

During dinner, James mentions the increase strength he feels deep inside himself, and Sharon mentions the same about the new-found Peace she now has.

"I know that comes from us now being joined as one. What's yours is mine, and what's mine is yours. The best part of the whole deal is now we know what Love has is now ours because we are now his," James says as he grabs Sharon and swings her around. Then they dance their way into the front room, laughing all the way.

As they settle down to talk, James looks at Sharon and asks, "What did you think of that Un story they told us?"

Sharon replies, "For such a little guy, he sure did cause a lot of trouble. I think Love is right. That is an excellent place to start shining the light about Love into peoples' lives. If you will speak, I will write, and together we shall put our plan of attack into motion."

Sharon goes to grab a pen and paper, while James proceeds to remember the words, which Love used to tell him about Un.

2

Un's Beginning

When Sharon returns, she sits and patiently waits for James to start speaking. She knows that he will only speak when he is very sure he has the truth lined up in the right order.

James turns to Sharon and begins, "Dear, there is so much. Tonight we shall start with the beginning. And after that, we shall add some more each day. First, let me put the definition of Un for reference. Un, according to *Webster*, means a prefix, freely used in English, to form verbs expressing a reversal of the same action or state. In other words, Un shows the opposite of the original."

"Now, shall we proceed with the story? From the very first, Love was here, and he made two children. One, out of the dust of the ground, a male child, which he called Adam. The other, he took a part out of Adam. You know, Love let Adam name the female, so Adam called her name Eve."

"Now according to Love, he had a wonderful time with his children and was teaching them many good things. He even gave them a universe to live in so they could learn to rule and reign. He gave them animals to take care of and plants for food to eat. There was only one condition Love gave to his children. That condition was to believe their father and not to eat of the tree of the knowledge of good and evil, which could also be called the tree of the truth and untruth.

"In every other way, Love put no conditions on his children. Love called this unconditional love for his children.

"Then one day, Un looked down, saw the Joy and Peace, Love's children, had with their belief in Love and became jealous. Un became lonely and decided to steal Love's children. You see, every time he got close to a word, it reversed and went the other way, away from Love. Since Un could not have belief, he decided to take theirs and change it.

"The only way to take them was to change their belief in the truth into unbelief. He had to make them do the only thing that Love had told them not to do. Therefore, Un set out to entice them with something that looked as if it was truth. But actually, Un was in front. Once they bit into the untruth, they were blinded from true belief and entered into the world of unbelief.

"Now, instead of Adam and Eve's world being full of unconditional love, they had entered the realm of conditions. Fear entered into their thoughts—fear that their father would think they were unlovable, unforgivable, and unredeemable. They had gone from feeling happy to being unhappy, righteous to unrighteous, worthy to unworthy, and desirable to undesirable."

James looks over through his tears and decides to take a break, for the tears are also running down Sharon's face just as fast. He knows she can no longer see to write.

Therefore, he takes her into his arms and softly says, "That is enough for now. Let's take a break, go for a walk, and get some fresh air. You know we have a long way to go to finish this story, but we are not required to get there tonight."

James and Sharon leave the house and take a long walk. When they return, the decisions are made: first a hot shower, then a good night's sleep.

They decide that first thing in the morning, they will take some time and go to the lot they have down at Tanglewood Lake. There they will start again on the story of Un.

3

More Un

After a wonderful night in each other's arms, James and Sharon awake with new strength to face another day. They head downstairs together. And while James call in to work for a few days off, Sharon goes and makes them some breakfast.

After eating, James helps Sharon make a list of the things they will need. The thought keeps going through their mind, with no phones and nobody knowing where they will be. The lake sound like the perfect, quiet place to be.

While Sharon packs clothes and food, James gathers bedding and fishing gear. Then they both pack the truck, and off they go.

The trip takes a while. And after they arrive at the lake, they proceed to set up camp. Then they grab a bite to eat.

With the necessities out of the way, James hands Sharon her pen and paper, asking her if she is ready to get started.

Sharon takes the pen and paper from James and says, "Whenever you are ready to start talking, I will be ready to start writing, my dear."

James looks at Sharon's notes, which she had taken last night, for a minute so to get his bearings. Then he continues, "Love knew that someday his children would eat of that tree. That is why he did not abandon his children. He even gave them a chance to tell him the truth. When he saw that Un had stepped in front of their belief and was blocking them from returning to him, he vowed to come and take them back someday.

"Love tried to reach out to his children in many different ways, but Un just kept attaching himself to Love's words more and more.

"Love gave me a list of words that Un got in front of. Un then twisted the truth, which Love's words contained. I think now would be a good place to put some of them. Love has been trying to tell his children, 'If only you would believe the words I send, then you could have them.'

"Love sent words like *faithful, joyful, loved, righteous, holy,* and many more, but Un kept getting in front of all of them."

Memories start flooding Sharon's mind with thoughts of how she was told she was unworthy, unfaithful, unholy, and unloved. She remembers not liking that feeling at all. She also remembers all the rules people had told her. One example she remembers so clearly, if you want to become holy, righteous, and worthy, then you must quit playing games, going to movies, and no cussing allowed. She heard, "You are to obey all these laws, which we will tell you to do."

Tears start falling from her eyes, and she looks at James to see he is crying right along with her. The words come out of her mouth before she even realizes they are on the march. "Damn that Un. I am glad Love defeated him."

James takes Sharon into his arms and speaks ever so softly, "He definitely is defeated, and that is what Love sent us to tell people. Finally, for all people who just believe there is a bridge, which Love built over that Un and back to Love."

Now, before we get ahead of the correct order, I think we should take a break and pull ourselves back together.

4

Love Is the Victory

After their break, James turns to his other half and says, "Now, we must tell the good news, which is that Love has won, just like he said he would.

"Now I think the best place to start this part is when Love found out what Un had done. Love, told Un, 'You might have bitten my heel, but I, Love, will come and crush your head, and I will take the blindness away from my children.

"That has happened. You see, when Un had thought he had killed Love—you remember that day, when Un had him nailed to the cross?—well, that is just what Love had planned.

You see, Love took all his children's wrongs and took them into his own flesh. Then willingly, Love laid down His life, for He knew, if it was willing, then He could pick his life back up again.

Then when Love stood back up, he took Un and put him back where Un belonged. Love became UNDEAD, never to die again, and offers that to all his children, if they will again just believe their Father and come back to Him."

James finds himself speaking very loudly as he announces, "Un is now UNDONE. Love finished the job he was sent to do."

Sharon also finds excitement flowing through her. Next thing she knows, she is standing up and shouting, "Hallelujah! Honey, Love gave us a wonderful mission. Now, I have understanding of the saying 'As a man think in his heart, so is he.' All of us have a House of Thoughts, which lives within.

"I now see why Mrs. Thought said to watch the path, for there are some thoughts we need to keep out of our house. But we still need to know they are outside, lurking on that path. That is why Love gives us thoughts to help us on all our journeys. We have been given the choice of truth or untruth. Love even asks us to choose the truth so that we may live."

James turns to Sharon, "There will be more missions, my dear. You know, I am looking forward to them. For now, let's just enjoy this one."

To My Readers

I pray you have enjoyed your trip to my House of Thoughts. I know I have enjoyed taking all who are willing to come with me.

Please remember what Love said, "I have not come to bring condemnation to anyone but to bring the truth."

Then through the truth, may love sets you free from all religious tradition. True love fulfills the whole law, and that is the will of God. Also, remember you have to receive before you have to give. We love because He first loved us.

The truth is, God is Love, and He came to set you free from Un. All you need to do is believe. Love has truly put Un back where Love meant for him to be. Therefore, hold tight the reins of truth and let your experiences with belief in what Love said to you lead you. Therefore, I beg you; do not give your reins to anyone except Truth, True Love.

The story you have just read is mostly true. I have changed some of the names in this story not to protect the innocent but so that the truth about love may shine.

You see, we all have our own House of Thoughts, and I have just taken you through mine. To some, their own House of Thoughts is too scary to go to. Maybe with me sharing mine, they may realize theirs do not have to be. Now I have found Love, Joy, and Peace flowing through my whole being. You see, by me going to my House of Thoughts along with Love's word called the Bible, Love helped me clean and rearrange my house. Now it is no longer a place where Fear and his group can come and stay. When you let Love fill your House of Thoughts, he really does flush out fear.

My motto for life:

> *I Am the Master's Piece In Progress. Any Complaints, See Master Please!*

Gifts for You

Below I list ten gifts for you
They're just waiting for receivers
These gifts are free, and this is true
So, step on up all you believers
Let us now start with number one
In Jesus we're God's daughter or son
Let us move on to number two
With Jesus we're no longer blue
Move on now to number three
In Jesus we find power to believe
Now we take in number four
In Jesus we find life means more
I'm looking now at number five
With Jesus, we find ourselves alive
Let's be quick and get onto six
In Jesus we learn now Satan's tricks
Now looking forward to number seven
In Jesus we find our ticket to heaven
What do you know here's number eight
With Jesus we'll go through a pearly gate
I'm now ready for number nine
In Jesus we find it's with God we dine
I hope you're ready for number ten
In Jesus we find it's us who win
God's word became flesh

About the Author

Yvonne Birnell is a wife to her wonderful husband, Terry; mother; grandma; and great-grandma. Only having a ninth-grade education that never held her back in her search for the truth, God blessed Yvonne with a love for words and hunger for truth.

Running from the God of Religious Institutions, which Yvonne had attended as a young lady yet searching for something to fill the longing in her soul, Yvonne Birnell started a journey to find the truth about Words and the power they have over our lives. Now Yvonne wishes to share her journey with you, her most memorable mission yet, *House of Thoughts*.

She is the author of *Poems from Within*.